D0175346

—A Contemporary Retelling
Of Charles M. Sheldon's Classic,
In His Steps —

WHAT WOULD JESUS DO?

Garrett W. Sheldon
Great-grandson of Charles M. Sheldon
WITH DEBORAH MORRIS

BROADMAN
& HOLMAN
PUBLISHERS

Nashville, Tennessee

THIS VOLUME IS DEDICATED TO THE GLORY OF GOD
and to all those who, through the power of the Holy Spirit,
seek to follow in His steps.

Printed in the United States of America

Unless otherwise noted, all Scripture quotations are from the Holy Bible, *New International Version,* copyright 1973, 1978, 1984 by International Bible Society.

ISBN 0-8054-6067-5

Preface

WHEN I WAS GROWING UP, MY FAMILY FREQUENTLY spoke of my grandfather, Rev. Charles M. Sheldon, and that he had written a religious book called *In His Steps*. I was told this book had sold more copies than any other religious book except the Bible, an estimated thirty million copies in fifteen languages worldwide. It was also something of a family joke that because of a faulty copyright my grandfather earned almost no money from this best-selling book, but that he didn't mind because he rejoiced that the message was so popular.

In His Steps was originally published in 1896, and it told the story of a group of people in a church that took a pledge to follow in Christ's steps by asking themselves in their daily lives, "What would Jesus do?"

The effects of that new discipleship are told through characters: a newspaper publisher, a woman singer, a businessman, young people. Each story emphasizes the vital importance of immediate, personal Christian action in our daily choices and decisions. It represents behavior informed by God's Word and the Holy Spirit toward family members, friends, co-workers, acquaintances, and strangers. They reveal a daily walk with our Savior's ways of reverence, love, peace, patience, humility, forbearance, reproachment, and forgiveness. The individuals in this story show the dramatic transformation in people's lives as they seek God's will in their lives and allow the Holy Spirit to live Christ's life through them.

I felt called to write an updated version of my grandfather's book for several reasons. One was a writer asking himself, *What would Jesus do in my place?* Another was my personal experience with the problems of the contemporary church and the realization that the question "What would Jesus do?" provided many solutions. The lifelong deepening of my Christian faith and life experiences that proved to me its truth fueled a desire to share its joys with others.

Many sources fed the awakening of that faith, including the writings of C. S. Lewis, the preaching of Charles Stanley, and the fellowship of many brothers and sisters in Christ. The realization came to me that after almost one hundred years, *In His Steps* could be updated with stories of contemporary Christians following obediently in Christ's footsteps.

My prayer is that it will bring something of God's saving grace to its readers and bless them with a hint of His glory.

Like the original book, *What Would Jesus Do*? is based on many actual events in the lives of believers but may not always represent specific living persons. My grandfather found inspiration for many of the stories in actual Christian endeavors in nineteenth-century America, and I have likewise instilled many of the characters in this book with real events of actual people following in the steps of Jesus. I know personally of hundreds of people who have turned their lives around, replacing joy for sorrow, peace for anxiety, love for hatred, fulfillment for emptiness, and service for bondage through a faithful walk with Jesus, indwelled by the Holy Spirit, obedient to our heavenly Father. To walk "in the steps" of Jesus is not only possible; it is a wonderful life-transforming reality for millions of Spirit-filled Christians around the world! Only recently, I heard from a lawyer and businessman on the West Coast whose life was enriched by applying the standard "What would Jesus do?" to his own business life. This new life of joyful Christian discipleship can be real for anyone who accepts Jesus as his or her Lord and Savior, seeks God's loving will through the knowledge of His Scriptures, the comfort and guidance of His Holy Spirit, and the love and support of true Christian fellowship in His church.

My mother's simple Baptist faith introduced me to God's saving grace early in my life. I am also grateful to my father, Charles M. Sheldon II, for his Christian witness and love, which have given me a taste of the heavenly Father's love for me. My wife Elaine's faith and witness have blessed my own Christian walk and contributed greatly to this book. My church family at Trinity Life Center Church in Coeburn, Virginia, and its pastors John and Martha McCarroll, have shown that a Spirit-filled, loving Christian fellowship can give one a taste of heaven. The Reverend Jim Collie, a dedicated Baptist Student Union campus minister and dear friend, gave unending encouragement and love. I felt that the Lord led me to publish this volume with Broadman & Holman and that has been confirmed by the wonderful care I have received by its staff, especially my editor Vicki Crumpton, whose kindness and skill have been a real blessing to this author.

To God be the glory.

GWS
Wise, Virginia
Spring 1993

Acknowledgment

MANY THANKS TO THOSE PEOPLE WHO WENT "THE extra mile" to contribute to this book by providing valuable glimpses into their professional lives, including Terry Mitchell, airport operations manager at Dallas's Love Field, and Ray Khalil, owner of the Southwest's popular "Swift-T" convenience store chain.

Also many thanks to pastor Keith Stewart, who contributed his prayers, insights, sermon notes, and fondness for alliterative message headings with unfailing good humor.

I

Michael Maxwell drew a deep breath and, glancing at the computer screen, read aloud the catchy sentence he'd just written: "Remember, the road to success is marked with many tempting parking places!" Even to his own ears, his rich baritone sounded convincing, warm, and personal with exactly the right touch of humor.

Then the phone rang—again. Although it was barely ten o'clock that overcast Friday morning, the busy minister's attempts to finish that week's sermon outline had been interrupted repeatedly.

Must be the weather, he thought in exasperation, wishing he'd remembered to turn on the answering machine. *I'll never finish if this keeps up.* When he answered the phone, however, he managed to keep the irritation out of his voice. "This is Michael Maxwell," he said. "What can I do for you?"

"Pastor Maxwell?" It was the breathless drawl of Lauren Woods, the attractive singles group coordinator at church. She'd recently volunteered to help with the mail ministry, an offer Michael suspected was motivated more by a desire to spend time with him than to see the church expand.

In his high-profile position at the prestigious First Church of Ashton, the handsome thirty-five-year-old had learned to take such displays of misplaced devotion in stride.

"Yes, Lauren?" he said shortly.

"I was working this morning on the advertising mailers for our next church concert," she began, "and I was wondering if . . ." Only half-listening, Michael fingered the ornate letter opener he'd bought in Spain the previous year, then narrowed his eyes to peer absently at the ceiling. This year, he and Sharon planned to vacation in Italy.

We both need a break, he thought. *Between our church schedule and fund-raising for the building committee, there's not been much time for anything else.*

Suddenly, he realized Lauren had asked him a question—something about ordering new mailing labels. "Uh, sure, that'll be fine," he replied hastily. "Keep up the good work." He put down the phone with relief, then switched on the answering machine before anyone else could call.

"That," he muttered, "is absolutely the last interruption I can stand this morning."

Sharon Maxwell, dark haired and stylishly dressed, had quietly entered the study. "I'm leaving now, so you'll have the house to yourself for a few hours. I have to go to the church to look at the fall curriculum for the preschool department." She smiled and bent to kiss her husband's cheek. "Need anything while I'm out?"

"Not that I can think of," Michael replied wearily, running his hand through his sandy brown hair. "I'm just going to sit here and try to finish my message notes for Sunday. If anybody else in the church has a crisis before lunch, they'll just have to call Dial-a-Prayer." They both laughed.

A few minutes later, in the soothing quiet of the empty house, Michael once again focused his attention on Sunday's sermon. He was on the next-to-last message of his latest series, "God's Steps to Success." His text for this week was 1 Peter 2:21:

To this you were called, because Christ suffered for you,
leaving you an example,
that you should follow in his steps.

His usual technique was to organize the message into an easy-to-follow outline, preferably with catchy subheadings. Today he had settled on "Discovery, Development, and Determination," drawing illustrations from the life of Christ to underscore the first two points. Now, with renewed enthusiasm, he started on the final point: "Determining to follow in Jesus' steps." He had just typed, "Three obstacles—Pride, Pain, Prejudice" when the doorbell pealed loudly.

Distracted, the minister shifted in his seat but didn't move to answer the door. When the bell rang a second time, however, he made an exasperated sound under his breath and stood up. Whoever it was, they weren't going away.

He was surprised to find a young, weary-looking black woman on his front step. Obviously pregnant, she appeared to be in her mid-twenties. She was gripping the hand of a well-scrubbed, but shabbily dressed, toddler.

"Are you the pastor of First Church?" she asked nervously. "Somebody told me he lived here."

"I'm Pastor Maxwell," Michael said slowly. "Is there something I can help you with?"

The woman stared up at him, taking in his rugged tanned features, his expensive shirt, his sharp green eyes. "I'm not really sure," she answered warily. "I need someone to watch my little girl."

Puzzled, the minister shook his head. "I'm sorry, but I don't know any baby-sitters. My wife and I don't have any children yet. Our church daycare center is just down the street; you might want to try there." He started to ease the door closed.

"Please," the woman said, a note of desperation in her voice. "You don't understand. I don't have any money to pay for daycare, and I already went to the church. They're the ones who sent me here."

Seeing his doubtful expression, she hurried on, "It would just be for a few weeks, until I got my first paycheck. I just got a job as a waitress downtown, but I can't take Hallie with me. I don't have anyone else to watch her."

Maxwell hesitated, unaccountably touched by the young woman's plight. But what could *he* do? "I really am sorry," he said sympathetically. "I wish I could help, but I don't know anybody who could do something like that. Would you like to leave your phone number in case I think of someone?"

She hesitated, but finally shook her head. She and the little girl turned away and started back toward the sidewalk. Michael gently closed the door and headed back to his study. The young mother's face lingered in his mind for a moment, but once he started working again, his absorption in the sermon quickly crowded everything else from his thoughts.

When Sharon returned home two hours later, she found her husband sitting on the edge of their bed, clad in gym shorts and pulling on tennis shoes. "Hi there," she greeted him. "I guess you finished your sermon. How did it turn out?"

"Pretty good," he replied. "I just hope we have better weather on Sunday than we've had the last few weeks. It's always easier to preach to big crowds."

He pulled his gym bag from the closet and tossed it onto the bed. "I'm going to the health club to work out for a few hours." He shifted his shoulders gingerly. "This sermon took a lot more work than it should have. I'm stiff all over!"

At dinner that evening, Sharon brought up the preschool's new plans for the fall. "They'll be using audio and video tapes to teach math and reading," she said. "It's all set to music. The smaller kids will just love it."

She suddenly paused. "Oh, that reminds me. I meant to tell you earlier, but while I was at the church a woman came in with a little girl, looking for child care. She was pregnant and seemed—I don't know—kind of distraught. Apparently she didn't have any money, so they couldn't help her. I felt really bad for her."

Michael glanced up. "I bet it was the same one who showed up here this morning. I guess she didn't have a husband, but I wonder where her family is? Surely they could help her out."

"You'd think so," Sharon said thoughtfully.

Sunday morning dawned bright and clear in Ashton. A warm, gentle breeze had swept up from the south, clearing away the last of the dark clouds and bringing with it the first hint of spring. As eleven o'clock approached, the enormous parking lot of First Church of Ashton was packed.

Inside, Daniel Marshall, the tall, graying president of Lincoln Christian College, greeted Dr. Patricia West, a tall, thirty-ish trauma surgeon quoted as an authority on several new emergency procedures. Jenny Paige, a fashionably dressed real estate developer in her late fifties, swept into the sanctuary with her son, Roger, who at twenty-four had inherited both her piercing blue eyes and her business acumen. Ted Newton, the wiry general manager of WFBB-TV, paused to shake hands with Alex Powell, a portly black man of military bearing who managed operations at Vickers Field Regional Airport. The First Church membership roster read like a "Who's Who" list of the most intellectual and affluent people in the city. The worship team at the front was just starting the pre-service performance, a contemporary instrumental version of "I Surrender All," including drums, piano, saxophone, synthesizer, and two electric guitars. It was a recognized signal for everyone to make their way to their seats.

The music at First Church rivaled many top professional Christian performances and was heavily advertised in the glossy brochures mailed to the community each month. The church held frequent concerts and had purchased a marquee-style billboard to place along the highway. It featured a tall picture of Michael and boldly proclaimed: *"Pastor Michael Maxwell Presents: Jesus!"* followed by that month's concert schedule.

Michael was aware that some people were drawn to First Church because of its sophisticated image, while others were offended by the church's contemporary thrust and slick advertising. He wasn't disturbed by the criticism.

"We have to get people in the door if we want them to hear the gospel," he insisted. "We're competing with the sports and entertainment industries and all their gimmicks. If it takes billboards or TV ads to get people's attention, that's okay." To keep the music top quality, the church had recently invested in a sound system that would make most concert halls envious.

At precisely eleven o'clock the worship team opened the service with prayer and led the congregation in several short choruses. Then the two lead vocalists, Rachel Wingate and Jason Clark, stepped forward to perform the morning's special.

The church instantly grew still. Rachel, twenty-two, could be a top magazine model with her curly, auburn hair and striking, gray-green eyes. Jason, two years older, was her perfect counterpart, tall and muscular with stylishly long, blond hair. Together they exuded an almost electric stage presence that left the congregation quivering with anticipation.

As the first strains of music started, Rachel spoke into her cordless microphone, "Pastor Maxwell will be delivering a message this morning about following Jesus. Jason and I would like to sing a song for you now about that subject, a remake of the old hymn 'Where He Leads Me I Will Follow.'"

Her comments ended at precisely the right moment in the musical introduction. After only the briefest of pauses she nodded at Jason, and with bright smiles they swept into the song:

I can hear my Savior calling,
I can hear my Savior calling,
I can hear my Savior calling,
"Take thy cross and follow,
follow me!"

As usual, the sweetness of their harmony literally drew gasps from the audience. Some people wiped their eyes and murmured, "Beautiful, just beautiful," while others, sensing the almost palpable link between the striking young couple, speculated about a future fairy-tale wedding. Rachel and Jason continued into the chorus:

Where He leads me I will follow,
Where He leads me I will follow,
Where He leads me I will follow,
I'll go with him, with him,
all the way.

When the last note tapered away, there was a thunderous round of applause, joined by Michael Maxwell as he took the pulpit. "Thank you, Rachel and Jason," he said warmly as the applause subsided. "After music like that, I'm not even sure I *need* to preach." The audience laughed appreciatively. After a few initial comments, Michael opened his Bible and began his sermon. He was exhilarated by the crowd's easy response that morning; as usual, the combination of music, comfortable seating and soothing surroundings had paved the way for his message. Although he avoided thinking of it in such terms, the careful staging of the Sunday morning services had played a large part in his ministerial success.

His sermon that morning was, as always, both stimulating and entertaining. Michael Maxwell loved standing in the pulpit, loved preaching the Word of God in ringing terms and observing the reaction of his widely-varied audience. He always included humorous stories and true anecdotes to keep his messages lively and was usually rewarded with comments like, "Excellent job, Pastor. The service just flew by." All in all, Michael was deeply satisfied with his life, his church, and his future.

Now, concluding the message, he closed his Bible and motioned for the worship team to proceed with the final chorus.

As he stepped out from behind the pulpit, however, he was startled by the sound of a shout from the audience. The shocked congregation turned to stare as a young black woman in the last row stepped out into the aisle and walked slowly toward the front, leading a small child by the hand.

With a jolt, Michael recognized his visitors from Friday. Before he could react they were standing at the front of the church. The woman's eyes looked red and tear-swollen, and as she turned to face the crowd she seemed to be moving in a feverish dream.

"I know you're not supposed to speak out in church," she said unevenly, "I'm sorry for interrupting, but I've reached the end of my rope. I don't have anywhere else to turn." Michael waved off two deacons who were striding purposefully toward the woman. He listened in dumb astonishment as she went on, "Six months ago when I found out I was pregnant again, my husband disappeared. I guess he didn't want to be bothered. I'd been taking computer programming classes at night, but after Jim left I had to drop out and go to work at a convenience store. My boss let me keep my daughter there with me, but then I got sick and they had to let me go. I got evicted from our apartment two weeks ago. Hallie and I have been living in my car ever since."

When she paused to take a shaky breath, Michael stole a glance at the silent congregation. Cliff Bright, the plump and balding owner of the "Mr. B Food Stores" chain, looked bewildered, his wife slightly irritated. Lauren Woods appeared horrified. Jason Clark and Rachel Wingate, seated on the front row, seemed riveted by the scene. Jason, embarrassed, suddenly shifted his eyes to the floor, but Rachel gazed on steadily at the woman with a deeply troubled expression. In the midst of the motionless crowd, her pale, intense face stood out as distinctly as if it had been framed in fire.

"The thing is," the woman continued, almost as if talking to herself, "I've been desperate these last few days. I didn't want charity, just someone to watch my daughter until I got my first paycheck. I called my parents, but they said God was punishing me for marrying someone like Jim. That's okay, I guess, but is He punishing my little girl too? Then I tried all the daycares, hoping I could work something out, but they just shook their heads. I guess I can't blame them; they've probably heard the same story before." She shut her eyes for a long moment, then opened them slowly. "I'm really sorry," she said wearily. "I shouldn't be bothering you people with my problems. But all this just doesn't make sense to me. What does it mean when people sing about 'surrendering all' and 'following Jesus'? I mean, I went to six different churches this last week looking for help, and your pastor here was one of the only people who'd even talk to me. He offered to take my phone number. That would have been great if I'd just had a phone. I thought—I always thought church people were supposed to act like Jesus—you know, 'doing unto others' and all that stuff. Isn't that right? But now it's too late, and I've lost the job—," she broke off in a sob, her lower lip trembling as she gazed down at her small daughter.

When she lifted her head again, her dark brown eyes were filled with despair. "I don't know what I'm going to do now. Where else can I go? I just wish—I really thought somebody would watch Hallie for just a few days, or at least give her a hot meal, so I could work. Isn't that what Jesus would do? *What would Jesus do?* I—I—" The woman lifted one trembling hand to her forehead, then, without warning, uttered a sharp exclamation of pain and doubled over, her face twisted with agony. When Michael leaped forward to steady her, she stared up at him without recognition, then with another gasping cry went limp in his arms.

A horrified murmur swept through the church. "Somebody call an ambulance!" Michael shouted.

The audience rose and crowded the aisles. Rachel Wingate impulsively stepped forward to help Michael lower the woman to the floor, then turned to comfort the frightened little girl. She was still cradling the child in her arms when Dr. Patricia West broke through the crowd and knelt beside the prostrate figure.

After a moment the tall surgeon looked up, her face grim.

"She's hemorrhaging," she said. "She needs to get to the hospital *fast*."

2

THE AMBULANCE LEFT FOR ASHTON MEMORIAL Hospital with the woman, tentatively identified as twenty-five-year-old Brenda Collier. Michael, more shaken than he was willing to admit, stood on the church steps talking with Alex Powell, Jason Clark, Jenny and Roger Paige, and several others who had lingered after the abruptly dismissed service. The child had remained behind with them, still clinging tearfully to Rachel.

"So what happens now?" asked Jason, glancing over at Rachel. He was more than a little surprised at her protective manner toward the little girl. She hadn't even seemed to notice the unsightly tear stains the sobbing child had left on the front of her jade silk dress.

Michael answered slowly, "Sharon and I are going to the hospital to see what we can do for her. It's the least we can do, since—" His voice trailed away, causing the others to look at him in surprise. They'd never seen their popular, well-spoken minister at a loss for words.

Rachel quietly stepped into the gap. "Pastor Maxwell, why don't I take the little girl home with me for now? I've got plenty of room in my apartment, and I'm on spring break from college right now." She paused, then added firmly, "I really wouldn't mind at all."

Jason looked surprised, and Roger Paige raised a questioning eyebrow. Rachel Wingate had never struck any of them as the motherly type. But Michael didn't question the young singer's offer. "Thanks, Rachel," he said. "That would be a big help."

At the hospital the Maxwells learned that Brenda Collier was in critical condition—and that due to the large amount of blood she'd lost, the child she'd carried had been stillborn. She hadn't awakened since her collapse at the church. They went to the waiting room and huddled together on the hard couch, distraught.

"If only I'd stepped in when she asked for help at the church," Sharon said brokenly. "Michael, how could I have ignored someone dying right in front of my eyes?"

But he was struggling with his own burden of guilt. "I was just as bad, or even worse. She practically begged me for help, but I turned her away because I was too busy preparing a sermon!" He laughed bitterly. "I can't believe this. Every time I think of her asking, 'What would Jesus do?' I'm condemned by my own words about following in His steps."

Deeply shaken, they began a prayerful vigil for the near-stranger lying in the Critical Care Unit.

Monday morning dawned with no change in Brenda's condition. Michael and Sharon had remained at the hospital throughout the long night; now they wearily walked downstairs to the cafeteria and bought cups of coffee. They had just sat down when they heard a familiar voice.

"Pastor Maxwell? Mrs. Maxwell?" It was Rachel, with little Hallie. She slipped into a chair beside them and lifted the child onto her lap. "I brought her to see her mommy. How is she?"

Sharon shook her head tiredly. "Not good, I'm afraid. She lost a lot of blood. They've given her transfusions, but she still isn't responding. The doctors aren't very encouraging."

Rachel was silent for a moment, taking in the information. Sharon studied the singer's pale face, suddenly realizing how odd it was that she had come to the hospital to check on the woman. Rachel had always avoided unpleasant situations, preferring to serve the church with her musical talents. Had she also been affected by the woman's desperate words, "What would Jesus do?"

Rachel leaned down to gently rest her cheek against Hallie's, her long, auburn hair vivid against the child's short, dark braids. "Can I help somehow? Have you already notified her family about what's happened?"

Michael shook his head. "We're still trying to find them. Yesterday we called the apartments where she used to live, but her neighbors didn't know much about her. The apartment manager said Brenda and her husband had moved from somewhere in the Southwest, but he didn't have any names or addresses. He thought Jim Collier had gotten into drugs in the last six months. He thinks he's probably still around here somewhere."

"But if he's taking drugs," Rachel murmured, looking down at Hallie, "we wouldn't let him take her, would we? I mean, if something happens to her mother?"

Sharon met her eyes. "Not if we can help it."

For the next twenty-four hours, the minister and his wife rarely left Ashton Memorial. Dr. West kept them posted on Brenda's condition and occasionally let them visit the unconscious woman. Hoping she might somehow be able to hear them, Michael and Sharon repeatedly assured her that little Hallie was being cared for.

Rachel had, in fact, been acting with surprising skill as a surrogate mother. After leaving the hospital the day before, she had taken Hallie shopping for some much-needed clothes and shoes at the nearby Ashton Square Mall. Strolling along hand in hand with the child, Rachel was mildly amused by the stares they drew from several matrons. She helped Hallie try on several new spring dresses at one store, then at another selected socks and underwear, a sunny yellow nightgown, a pair of flowered shoes, and after a moments thought, a wide plastic hair pick, baby shampoo, and hair conditioner specially made for coarse black hair.

"Now all I have to do is figure out how to fix your hair back in all those little braids once I wash it," she told Hallie as they waited to check out.

"I have a feeling it's harder than it looks." The little girl, understanding Rachel's warm tone if not her words, bounced up and down and said appealingly, "Up!" Rachel smiled and picked her up, leaning her forehead against Hallie's for a moment.

"I love you, little one," she whispered, her eyes glistening with tears as she thought of the young woman silently fighting for her life at Ashton Memorial.

What would become of her daughter if she died?

It was late that Tuesday afternoon, as Michael and Sharon sat in the hospital waiting room, that Dr. West looked around the corner. A moment later the trauma surgeon entered the room with a staff physician, Dr. Kenneth Bender.

The Maxwells looked up, correctly interpreting their solemn expressions. Sharon said softly, "She's gone, isn't she?"

Dr. West nodded, seeming unable to speak. Dr. Bender cleared his throat. "Has anyone located her family yet?"

Michael shook his head. "We're still trying. But if we can't find them quickly, the church will take responsibility for the arrangements."

Over the next few days, as word spread of the tragedy, the church office was flooded with calls. In Michael Maxwell's ten years at First Church of Ashton, he had never witnessed such an outpouring of concern for a stranger. It was as if the church had suddenly awakened from a numbing sleep.

On Thursday, Jim Collier was finally located in a Chicago suburb, living with a seventeen-year-old girl. Although he claimed to be shocked at the death of his wife and child, he balked at making the two-hour drive to Ashton to make funeral arrangements—or even to provide for his daughter's care.

"No man in his right mind could be that callous. I have to believe it was drugs talking," Michael told Sharon afterwards. "But at least I got a phone number from him for Brenda's parents in Arizona."

Mr. and Mrs. Anderson took the news of their daughter's death much harder than their son-in-law had.

"Brenda didn't tell us she was pregnant," Mrs. Anderson said tearfully, "or that she'd been evicted from her apartment. She just said Jim had left her again and she needed to drop out of school and go back to work. We'd helped her out before, but each time she got back on her feet, Jim showed up again, and she took him back. This time I was furious with her. I told her she was getting what she deserved for marrying a man like that!"

Michael tried to comfort them, but it was a distressing conversation. They said they would fly into Ashton the next day to arrange for their daughter's body to be brought back to Arizona, and also to pick up their small granddaughter.

"Thank you, pastor, for calling us," Mr. Anderson said brokenly. "So few people are willing to become involved these days, even so-called Christians. That's one reason my wife and I quit going to church years ago." He drew a shaky breath. "I think now maybe that was a mistake."

Over the days that followed, Michael faced an agonizing time of prayer and self-examination. How, he asked himself miserably, had he drifted so far from his beginnings in the ministry? He had started out earnestly wanting to touch people's lives, but as his success had grown, so had his responsibilities. For the last five years his "job description" at First Church had more closely resembled that of a corporate CEO than a pastor.

Dear Lord, he prayed, *please take me back to the basics. Teach me what it truly means to be Your disciple.*

That Sunday morning dawned on the city of Ashton exactly as the Sunday before. The air was fresh and clean, scented with the first spring flowers. Michael Maxwell entered his pulpit to face one of the largest congregations that had ever crowded into First Church.

The service started quietly that morning. The worship team led a few simple songs but omitted the usual musical special. The subdued feeling among those in the service resulted in only a half-hearted attempt at applause as the musicians took their seats. Rachel Wingate had noticeable dark circles under her eyes.

Now, as Michael gazed out over the congregation, he seemed curiously hesitant. His usual quick smile was missing, and there was an uncomfortable silence as he laid out his notes and opened his Bible. Several church members exchanged glances; their handsome young pastor looked almost ill.

Michael cleared his throat. "We'll conclude our series on 'God's Steps to Success' this morning with the message, 'Believing and Achieving,'" he said slowly. "But before we begin, please join with me in prayer."

As he closed his eyes and began to ask God's blessing on the service, Brenda Collier's face suddenly rose to his mind with vivid clarity. A painful lump constricted his throat as he heard again her desperate challenge, "What would Jesus do?"

His voice abruptly faltered. "Above all, heavenly Father," he prayed, "show us this morning what it really means to follow in Your steps. In Jesus' name we pray, amen."

The sermon that followed was far from eloquent. Twice Michael lost his place in his notes and had to go back over a point to make it clear. It was evident that some idea which had little to do with that morning's message struggled in his thoughts for expression.

Finally, toward the end of the service, the minister seemed to make a decision. Closing his Bible, he stepped out from behind the pulpit to face the congregation.

"Last week," he said with a sudden strength painfully absent from his earlier message, "a young woman named Brenda Collier stood up in our morning service to tell how she'd gone to various churches and businesses here in Ashton asking for help but each time had been turned away. She wondered what we Christians mean when we sing songs like 'I Surrender All,' when in fact, we seem to surrender very little. Then she posed a very simple question: 'What would Jesus do?' For those of you who haven't yet heard, she passed away Tuesday afternoon at Ashton Memorial Hospital. The child she was carrying at that time was stillborn."

Michael paused and looked out over the congregation; he'd never seen so many earnest faces. Jenny Paige fixed her sharp blue eyes on him, her expression unreadable; beside her, even cynical young Roger was unusually attentive. *How can I adequately express what I am feeling?* Michael thought. "Jesus made it clear that we demonstrate our love for Him by how we treat those around us in need. Most of us know the passage in Matthew:

'I was hungry and you gave me something to eat,
I was thirsty and you gave me something to drink,
I was a stranger and you invited me in,
I needed clothes and you clothed me,
I was sick and you looked after me,
I was in prison and you came to visit me.'

Then the righteous will answer him,
'Lord, when did we see you hungry and feed you,
or thirsty and give you something to drink?
When did we see you a stranger and invite you in,
or needing clothes and clothe you?
When did we see you sick or in prison and go to visit you?'

The King will reply,
'I tell you the truth, whatever you did for one of the least
of these brothers of mine, you did for me.'

Then he will say to those on his left,
'Depart from me, you who are cursed,
into the eternal fire prepared for the devil and his angels.

For I was hungry and you gave me nothing to eat,
I was thirsty and you gave me nothing to drink,
I was a stranger and you did not invite me in,
I needed clothes and you did not clothe me,
I was sick and in prison and you did not look after me.'

They will also answer
'Lord, when did we see you hungry or thirsty
or a stranger or needing clothes or sick or in prison,
and did not help you?'

He will reply,
'I tell you the truth, whatever you did not do for one of
the least of these, you did not do for me.'"
Matthew 25:35-45

Pain was apparent in the strained lines of Michael's face. "Few of you know this, but Brenda Collier actually came to my door asking for help. She was a stranger—and I didn't invite her in. She was hungry—I didn't feed her. She needed clothes—but I didn't offer any. I didn't realize it at the time, but in turning her away, I turned away my Lord."

He stopped, groping for the right words. "I've done a lot of praying and soul-searching these last few days, and I've come to some difficult conclusions. No church program, no matter how well done, can touch other people as powerfully as individual acts of compassion.

"I wasn't planning to do this today, but I can't think of any better time than now to share an idea that's gradually been forming in my mind."

In the audience Alex Powell suddenly sat up straighter, his square features projecting a determined attentiveness. Across the church Ted Newton nervously ran his fingers through his thick, wavy hair, looking puzzled but alert. Cliff Bright leaned slightly forward, his plump face expectant. When his wife frowned and touched his arm, he settled back but kept his eyes on the pastor.

Michael wondered, as he studied their faces, how many would respond to the proposal he was about to make. He plunged on, choosing his words carefully.

"What I'm going to suggest now shouldn't seem strange or fanatical, but I'm sure that at least some of you will see it in that light. I'll put it to you bluntly: I want volunteers from First Church who will, along with me, commit for one full year to take no action without first asking the question, 'What would Jesus do?'"

Michael paused, half expecting some audible reaction from the audience. But they sat frozen, every eye fixed intently on his face.

"After asking yourself that question, those of you who take this pledge will attempt to follow Jesus as best you know how, no matter what the consequences. After the service today, I will be in the lecture room to talk with everyone willing to join me in taking such a pledge."

He took a deep breath and let it out slowly. The paralyzed congregation began to stir, some members glancing at each other in astonishment. It wasn't like Michael Maxwell to suggest such a radical idea.

Three rows back, a secretary named Terri Bannister stared sightlessly at her burgundy leather Bible, considering the minister's challenge. She'd been attending First Church for two years now with her three children, despite her husband's scornful disapproval of "religious brainwashing." How would he react if she took such a pledge?

Directly behind her, Lauren Woods was also looking thoughtful. Deep in her heart there was a sudden stirring, an almost forgotten longing for—what? Was it possible the emptiness in her life was actually a yearning to walk with God Himself?

Michael closed the service in prayer, and then the worship team began to play softly. Rachel Wingate was noticeably missing from the front, as was Jason Clark. As the sanctuary began to empty, animated groups stood around talking about the pastor's radical proposition. Michael said good-bye to several visitors, then headed toward the lecture room.

He paused just outside the door, wondering who, if anyone, had responded to the challenge. Out of all the affluent and sophisticated members of First Church, he could think of less than a dozen men and women whose Christian commitment might lend itself to such a dramatic move. Uttering a silent prayer, he entered the room.

He was startled to find perhaps fifty people waiting. He glanced around, noting with some astonishment that along with Sharon and several dedicated members like Alex Powell and Daniel Marshall were some others he'd consider extremely unlikely to participate under the circumstances: Ted Newton, Jenny Paige, Rachel Wingate, Dr. West, and Jason Clark.

When the minister walked to the front, a hush fell over the crowd. He turned to face them, his strong face plainly revealing the depth of emotion he felt. Michael hadn't realized until that very moment what an overwhelming love he had for these earnest-faced men and women. His eyesight momentarily blurred, and he was forced to bow his head to regain control before he spoke. "Will you please pray with me?" he asked quietly.

"Lord, we are gathered here today to begin a great adventure with You. We don't know where it will take us, and we feel a little uncertain about the future, but we trust You to guide us in this endeavor step by step."

From the very first word he uttered, the almost tangible presence of the Holy Spirit filled the room, touching them all. As the prayer went on, this Presence grew in power, bringing tears to many people's eyes. If an audible voice had spoken from heaven to bless the bold step they were taking, not one person present would have felt any more certain of God's approval.

When the prayer ended there was a silence that lasted several minutes. Michael slowly looked up, seeing his own sense of wonder reflected in Sharon's eyes, as well as in the faces of many of the others. For a moment he couldn't speak.

"As you know," he finally said with difficulty, "I've been forced this past week to face some very unpleasant truths about myself. Somewhere along the line, I started substituting programs and church activities for personal involvement with people. I could make up excuses for it, but the fact is, *it's not what Jesus would do.*

"So, as I announced this morning, I have determined for the next year, starting today, to live every day by asking myself, 'What would Jesus do?' Once I decide to the best of my ability what action He would take in a specific situation, I will try to follow through, regardless of the consequences.

"This is the pledge I'm making before you and before God. I'm glad many of you decided to join me."

There was a quiet but unanimous murmur of assent. Michael asked, "Are there any questions?"

Rachel Wingate raised her hand. "Pastor Maxwell," she said hesitantly, "I'm not really sure how I'm supposed to figure out what He would do in my place. I mean, life today is nothing like it was in Bible times."

Michael nodded. "I don't have a quick answer to that," he admitted, "but I know that if we pray and ask for guidance from the Holy Spirit, we'll have it. Remember what Jesus said?

'But when he, the Spirit of truth, comes,
he will guide you into all truth.
He will not speak on his own;
he will speak only what he hears,
and he will tell you what is yet to come.'"

John 16:13-15

"But what if someone else thinks Jesus would do something differently than you're doing it?" asked Daniel Marshall, thinking of the differing opinions expressed among the professors and theologians at Lincoln Christian College.

"You can't help that. But as long as we all do our best to follow Jesus' example as closely as possible, I can't believe there'll be too much confusion. The important thing is, once we ask the Spirit to tell us what Jesus would do and receive an answer, we have to act on it, regardless of the consequences to ourselves. Are we agreed?"

Everyone nodded, and Michael felt a growing sense of joy. *I don't know where all this will take us,* he thought in excitement, *but I'm certain this is the right thing to do.* After talking for a few more minutes, they agreed to meet in the lecture room again the following Sunday.

Alex Powell closed in prayer, and again the Spirit manifested Himself in power and love. Heads remained bowed a long time, and when the group slowly stood up to leave, there was a feeling of awe that prevented speech. Sharon walked outside with Rachel Wingate and Lauren Woods.

After the room cleared, Michael retreated to his office and knelt beside the couch to pray. He remained there by himself for almost an hour, unaware that he and First Church would soon witness the most remarkable series of events the city of Ashton had ever known.

3

Ted Newton walked through the doors of Channel 5, WFBB-TV, on Monday morning with a new, but still unformed, resolve. Although the tall, energetic station manager had stayed after church Sunday largely on impulse, he had been firm in taking the pledge to make decisions only after asking, "What would Jesus do?" Now, as he considered what that might mean in the days and weeks ahead, he felt both excited and apprehensive.

Arriving a few minutes early, he sat down at his desk and automatically glanced at his appointment calendar. As usual, it was packed solid. But this time, instead of immediately plunging into the day's tasks, Ted got up and closed his door. Feeling distinctly awkward, he knelt beside his desk on the plush carpet and silently asked the Holy Spirit to direct him that day.

Then he got up, switched on the TV monitor bank that stretched along one wall of his office, and settled back in his comfortable leather chair to read the "overnights," the area-wide ratings from the previous day's programming. Every few minutes, he glanced up to scan the TV screens which simultaneously monitored Channel 5 and four of its biggest Chicago competitors. As president and general manager of the local network affiliate, it was his responsibility to make sure their station consistently captured a major share of the market.

This morning the overnights looked good; their prime-time programming the previous evening had drawn an 18 rating and 31 percent share, and they'd shown a healthy profit. In a gesture familiar to those who worked with him, Ted ran his fingers nervously through his hair and bent closer to compare their performance with the competition's. With another "sweeps" period on the horizon, it was crucial that advertisers saw Channel 5 as *the* place to buy air time.

He was still studying the ratings sheet when the program director tapped on the door and stuck his head inside.

"Do you have time to talk about that 'Wednesday's Child' special for next week?" Keith Walton asked. "I need to know if we're going to preempt the network programming to air it."

Ted smiled and waved him in. "This is probably as good a time as any. Have a seat."

Keith settled himself comfortably into a chair, admiring the office's expensive decor. Lush green plants were positioned near the plate glass window, and the textured walls were adorned with various impressionist paintings and plaques. A small, framed picture of Newton's smiling, blond wife and twelve-year-old daughter was propped by his appointment calendar. His mahogany desk was scattered with engraved paperweights and mementos presented to him for years of community service.

"Looking at our lineup for next Wednesday," Keith said, "I think it would be a major mistake to bump 'Lexa' to air a show about abused children who need homes. We're already struggling in that time slot, and a depressing show like that might send us down even farther."

Ted considered it briefly. "I think you're right. Let's stay with the scheduled programming."

"Sounds good."

The program director was almost to the door when Ted suddenly said, "Keith? Just a minute."

It had struck him belatedly that he'd made the decision without any thought to the pledge he had taken. Now, with a conscious effort, he silently asked himself, *What would Jesus do in this situation?*

"On second thought," he said slowly, "I think maybe we should run 'Wednesday's Child' after all. We'll preempt 'Lexa' this time and hope for the best."

"But why?" Keith asked, puzzled.

"That's my decision. Let production know, will you?"

"But—," the program director stared at his boss in astonishment. "But Ted, that's just—"

The general manager cut him off with a placatory gesture. "I guess I owe you an explanation," he said. "Come back in and close the door."

When Keith sat back down, Newton looked at him appraisingly. The program director attended a small fellowship on the outskirts of Ashton's south side, a blighted residential area generally avoided by the larger churches. Although the two men had worked together at the station for over three years and enjoyed a comfortable relationship, they had never discussed religious issues.

That was about to change.

"Keith," Ted said, "if Jesus Christ were the general manager of Channel 5, do you think He would run a talk show about—," he flipped through several papers and continued,

"'Older Women, Younger Men,' in place of a special that might help needy children find adoptive homes?"

Keith laughed. "You're kidding, right?"

"No, I'm really not," Ted responded mildly. "What do you think He would do?"

"Probably run 'Wednesday's Child.' But—"

"There are no 'buts.' I made a commitment yesterday not to make any decisions for the next year without first asking myself, 'What would Jesus do?' That's the reason for my decision."

Keith slumped in his chair, looking a little dazed. "If this gets back to the Broadcast Division, they're going to explode. I mean, I'm all for it, but do you honestly think this station can operate successfully like that? People want to be entertained, not preached at. In an ideal world, doing the right thing would always pay off—but this isn't an ideal world. We'll lose viewers, and advertisers will pull their accounts." He gave Ted a sharp look. "You'll lose your contract."

Ted nodded slowly. "If we start losing viewers, that's exactly what will happen. But," he added, "I can't help but think that at least some people will appreciate an attempt on our part to show increased integrity in what we air. We might do better than ever!"

Keith, still skeptical, muttered darkly, "I hope you're right."

Leaving Newton's office, the program director wore a bewildered look, like a man who'd stumbled by accident into a stranger's house. He was both impressed and shaken by his boss's unlikely decision to run the station by a higher standard. It was risky—but what an incredible adventure it could be if it succeeded!

As he made his way back to his own department, however, he shook his head. *It won't work,* he thought glumly. *I just hope he doesn't take the rest of us down with him.*

Ted was struggling with the same thought. Having made the decision, he was willing to bear the personal consequences of his actions. But was it fair to involve station employees like Keith in a venture that might prove to be disastrous?

What would Jesus do?

He pulled out a sheet of paper and, after a moment's hesitation, wrote neatly across the top:

What Jesus Might Do in Ted Newton's Position

1. He wouldn't pressure subordinates to support His decisions, only to comply with them. He would make it clear that any protests they voiced would not jeopardize their positions in any way.

2. If the public reacted negatively to the programming changes, He would openly take the blame.

I could let the Ashton Herald *television critic know I'd made the changes over my program director's protests,* Ted thought wryly. *That would get the word out quickly enough.* He paused, his eyes straying to the picture of his small family. Kim and Ashley had left right after church to go shopping for Ashley's school orchestra dress and had missed the meeting about the First Church pledge. How would they react if his actions cost him his job? After a moment he continued, his face grave:

3. If it became apparent that the attempt to profitably run Channel 5 by the standard of asking, "What would Jesus do?" was failing, and that the company was losing money due to His personal commitment, He would offer to voluntarily terminate His two-year contract and resign as president and general manager.

Ted sighed. Now, if Keith Walton was proved right in his gloomy assessment, no one but Ted himself would suffer.

4

THE PRE-DAWN AIR WAS DAMP AND CHILLY, THE SKY gray, as Alex Powell strode briskly through the airport employee parking garage. Reaching the elevator, he pressed the call button, straightening his sports coat and tie as he waited. This crisp Wednesday morning already held the promise of turning into a long and difficult day.

Powell, a broad-shouldered black man in his late fifties, managed the Vickers Field Operations Division. He stepped through the elevator doors, pressed "2," then waited as the mechanism creaked and groaned its way slowly upward. The regional airport, built almost forty years earlier, was definitely feeling its age.

And so am I, thought Alex ruefully, rubbing one graying temple as he thought of the day ahead. *Until we decide how to fix the noise problem out at the runup building, I'm going to do nothing but sit in meetings.*

Still musing, Powell stepped out onto the second floor, waving at Maggie, a young woman on the custodial crew. She shyly returned his wave before bending back to her task of cleaning a water fountain.

Entering the airport operations department, Alex paused to pour himself a cup of coffee before heading back to his own rather small office. Vickers Field, although far larger than many regional airports, was still modest by comparison to Chicago's O'Hare International, only forty-five minutes away by commuter flight. But the advantages of working at Vickers—less bureaucracy and more ability to have a personal impact—more than compensated for the cramped office space.

Powell lowered himself into his desk chair and, coffee mug in hand, picked up the daily report: two stapled pages detailing weather conditions, maintenance or custodial problems, airport activities and an inspection checklist. Scanning down the pages, he was relieved to see that no "139s"—serious problems requiring immediate action—had occurred since he'd left the previous evening.

The few problems listed were simple ones: (1) Light out above Grey Aero Tech hangar; (2) Clocks in main terminal not reset for daylight saving time. Chuck Finley, Powell's managerial counterpart in Facilities, had probably already dispatched workers to correct those items.

Finley, a licensed engineer, managed the airport's maintenance, repair, and custodial crews, while Powell was in charge of overall operations: inspections, security, emergency rescue crews, and ground transport. There were times, however, when their responsibilities overlapped, causing tension between them. It was part of Powell's job to make frequent inspection tours of the airport operations areas, noting repair or maintenance problems like pitted taxiways or peeling paint. The facilities manager often took his meticulous reports personally.

"Do you have to pick on *every* tiny detail?" Finley frequently demanded. "Are you just trying to make me look bad?" He was only slightly mollified by Alex's assurances that he was just doing his job.

Now, as Alex prepared to work his way down the list of noise and security issues he needed to discuss with the airport board, he paused, as he did most mornings, to silently commit his day to the Lord. It was a habit he had formed years before during a difficult recovery from alcoholism. That experience had taught him, far more effectively than any sermon, how to rely on God's presence in his daily life. He credited it with holding his marriage together during those painful months.

Despite his strong commitment, however, Alex had been intrigued by Michael Maxwell's challenge. Was it possible, he wondered, that he had fallen into comfortable Christian routines that had left him blind to the needs of those around him? Was he truly living as Jesus would in his place?

Open my eyes, he now prayed simply, *and show me how to imitate You today.*

The morning passed quickly. Powell and Finley met briefly to discuss several minor maintenance problems, and then they decided to break for lunch.

A surprisingly good Italian restaurant, "Ciccio's," was located in the airport. Standing in the cafeteria line, Powell spotted Maggie and an older woman on the custodial crew sitting down at a corner table. As he watched they started spreading out home-packed lunches. Almost instantly, the restaurant manager swooped down on their table. His deep voice carried across the small room.

"I'm sorry," he said icily, "but you can't bring your lunches in here. You need to go to the employee break room."

Maggie looked embarrassed. "But we bought drinks here, and I bought a salad. I'd rather skip lunch than eat in that break room. It's so gloomy and filthy it makes me lose my appetite."

The man gave her a haughty look. "Then why don't you clean it? Aren't you good at that job?"

Maggie hastily began to gather her lunch and help her friend with hers. She jumped when Alex Powell suddenly appeared and towered over the table.

"Have a seat," he told Maggie firmly, then turned to the manager. "These two ladies will be my guests for lunch today."

Finley, just behind him, took in the scene with thinly-veiled astonishment. What was Alex thinking to invite two *janitors* to sit with them?

Powell took a seat, noting Finley's disapproval with wry amusement. "You don't have to sit with us," he said dryly. "I see Roger in line; he'll probably be looking for a table in just a minute."

"Actually, I had something I needed to discuss with him anyway, and this *would* be the perfect time. Sure you don't mind?"

"Not at all. Good talking to you, Chuck."

Alex watched the facilities manager retreat to the safety of the other table, then turned to smile encouragingly at Maggie and her friend. In their weary faces he found all the assurance he needed that he'd done the right thing.

You acted on My behalf, a still, small voice seemed to whisper. *Well done, My good and faithful servant.*

That afternoon, before he left for home, Alex Powell made an unaccustomed diversion to the employee break room in the basement. Walking in slowly, he noted the peeling linoleum, the dirty green walls devoid of any decoration, and the water-stained ceiling tiles. The metal table legs were rusted and the vinyl seat cushions were cracked with age. The only "luxury" in the room—a single soda machine—had an Out of Order sign taped across it. He stood there for several minutes, lost in thought. It was only gradually that an exciting idea began to stir at the back of his mind.

5

It was Sunday morning, and First Church of Ashton was crowded once again. There was excitement in the air, a kind of breathless anticipation as the time drew near for the service to begin. Even the worship team seemed to feel it. As they started playing the morning prelude, several instrumentalists closed their eyes, focusing their attention on the Lord rather than the audience. A sweet spirit seemed to fill the church and the hearts of those gathered there.

Ted and Kim Newton were talking quietly when Dr. Patricia West came in and looked around the sanctuary. Recognizing the station manager from the after-church meeting the previous Sunday, she smiled and extended her hand.

"How has your week been?" she asked, broadening her smile to include Kim. "For me, it's definitely been a strange seven days."

Ted returned her handshake, then introduced Kim. "I know what you mean," he said excitedly. "I felt like I woke up Monday morning in a whole new country where I had to rethink even my simplest decisions. It's odd, though; I feel better, less stressed, than I have in years. It's nice to know that if I follow Jesus, it's *His* job to worry about the future."

Kim reacted to her husband's words by shooting a sharp glance in his direction. After fourteen years of marriage, she thought she knew Ted well. He'd always been outgoing and impulsive, a "workaholic" who wasn't happy unless he had several projects going at one time. He was usually miserable on vacations, anxious to get back to the station.

For the past week, though, he'd been acting—well, strange. He kept talking about this "pledge" he had taken and trying to convince her to stay after church this week with him to hear about it. They'd been discussing it—arguing, really—when the doctor interrupted. Kim wanted to understand, but she was deeply disturbed. What if this new idea of Ted's compromised his position at Channel 5?

Across the sanctuary, Jenny Paige, Alex Powell, and his wife, Cheryl, were also talking about their experiences. Jenny, her silver hair loosely gathered in an elegant knot, had chosen a seat beside the Powells near the front of the church. Roger also sat with them, but appeared more interested in scanning the congregation for potential business contacts than in his mother's conversation.

The Powells were both animated, so obviously excited about something, that Jenny finally asked in amusement, "What's happening that I don't know about?"

Alex laughed. "It's probably not all that exciting, but it looks like an idea I had this last week is going to work out." He went on to explain, "I just talked with Pastor Maxwell, and he's agreed to come to Vickers Field to lead a twice-weekly Bible study before hours in the employee break room. I cleared it with the director of Aviation, and I also talked him into having the break room refurbished to make it a decent place for the work crews to relax."

Jenny looked thoughtful. "Do you think any of the workers will actually show up for a Bible study?"

"Eight people already said they'd come, and that they'd bring others."

Cheryl smiled. "He hasn't been this excited about work in a long time. I think he'd be out at Vickers Field today if I'd let him!"

Just then the service started.

After the opening prayer and choruses, Michael Maxwell stepped up and laid his Bible on the pulpit, but he didn't immediately start into the message. Instead, he looked out over the congregation with a sudden, deep stirring of compassion, the feeling of a loving shepherd for his flock. The wrenching intensity of his emotions left him momentarily unsettled.

"Today," he finally began, "I'll be preaching a message titled 'God's Wake-Up Call.' For some of you it will only reinforce what you've experienced this past week; for others, it will probably seem overly blunt or even offensive. All I can tell you is that I honestly believe, in keeping with the pledge I made last week, that this is what Jesus would preach in my place."

The sermon that followed was dramatically different from those he had preached in the past. Rather than using clever phrases to appeal to his listeners' intellects or delivering a calculated "feel-good" message, he wielded God's Word to strip away systematically all the sophisticated excuses for lives ruled by lust, greed, or selfish ambition.

"Jesus was known as a friend of sinners," he said. "He offered mercy and forgiveness to thieves, adulterers, even murderers. He reserved His harshest words for 'religious' people: self-righteous churchgoers who lived by their own rules, who often painlessly gave to noble causes but turned a deaf ear to the poor and helpless on their own doorsteps. He had a name for those people. He called them 'hypocrites.'"

There was a long moment of silence as the full implication of his words swept across the congregation. Some faces showed shock and indignation. Just who was Pastor Maxwell accusing of hypocrisy? The very people who paid his salary every week? Several exchanged glances, already planning their irate comments once the service ended.

Others' faces, however, held a solemn acknowledgment of the truth—and even more, a hunger for guidance. Like the young man who cried, "What must I do to be saved?" they waited to hear what they should do to be counted worthy of the name "Christian."

Michael continued, "In the Gospel of Mark, Jesus said this:

'If anyone would come after me, he must deny himself and
take up his cross and follow me.
For whoever wants to save his life will lose it, but
whoever loses his life for me and for the gospel will save it.

'What good is it for a man to gain the whole world,
yet forfeit his own soul?
Or what can a man give in exchange for his soul?
'If anyone is ashamed of me and my words
in this adulterous and sinful generation,
the Son of Man will be ashamed of him
when he comes in his Father's glory with the holy angels.'
Mark 8:34-38

"I believe the time has come for us to ask ourselves some hard questions. In this self-serving age when most of us are reluctant to forgo any luxury or desire, what, on a practical level, have we denied ourselves? What cross have we borne for Christ's sake? What suffering have we willingly endured?" He looked out over the congregation, vaguely aware of Alex Powell's slight nod and Cliff Bright's thoughtful gaze. There was a hushed stillness across the sanctuary, an almost holy sense of reflection. *Please, Lord,* Maxwell prayed, *let this message reach their hearts.*

"God's wake-up call for some of us might be to put aside an expensive vacation or new car and follow Him in giving to those in need; for others it might be to sacrifice our social standing in order to speak out against moral compromise. The 'cross' you are called to bear will probably be different from mine and from that of your neighbor's.

"But the fact is, if you're a Christian, you have been called by God to embark on an incredible adventure, an 'abundant life' that involves both joy and sacrifice. How many are willing to accept that calling? How many would rather stay comfortably asleep, untouched by the world that's dying around us?"

His ringing words hung in the air, reverberating as a living sword of truth that pierced the very hearts and souls of those who listened. When he led in prayer, some who had never before wept in church found their faces wet with tears.

To close the service, Rachel Wingate stood up to sing. Her voice rose, strong and sweet, in a quiet hymn of praise, but this time something was different. She wasn't "performing"; she was rejoicing in God's goodness. Her lovely face was transformed, all traces of her former vanity gone. The audience instinctively sensed the change without fully understanding it.

Michael asked those who had remained after the service the previous week to briefly meet again in the lecture room and also invited any others willing to take the pledge to join them. After speaking with a few visitors, he hurried back to the lecture room. He noted without comment that some long-standing members—including Martha Robinson, the church treasurer—had formed a small, unhappy group in the lobby. Several of them, seeing his glance, quickly looked away.

The crowd in the lecture room had almost doubled this time. Michael moved among them murmuring joyful greetings. He saw that Kim Newton had come with Ted this time, although she appeared uncomfortable. In the far back he spotted Cliff Bright, without his wife's company. The plump store owner looked both miserable and determined.

Michael made his way over to him and clasped his hand warmly. "Glad to see you, Cliff," he said quietly. "I guess Elizabeth didn't want to come?" Cliff shook his head. "She didn't want *me* to come either. I wanted to last week, but—" His round face bore a look of pain and sorrow that brought to Michael's mind Jesus' words:

> "I did not come to bring peace, but a sword. . . . 'A man's enemies will be the members of his own household.'
>
> "Anyone who loves his father or mother more than me
> is not worthy of me;
> anyone who loves his son or daughter more than me
> is not worthy of me;
> and anyone who does not take his cross and follow me
> is not worthy of me."
>
> Matthew 10:34, 36-38

As before, Michael opened with prayer. And as before, the Holy Spirit swept through the room. Afterward, the group talked informally, asking questions and comparing experiences.

Alex Powell shared his news about the employee Bible study beginning at the airport. "I believe that in my place Jesus would be concerned about the employees, both spiritually and physically. It'll be easier for them to believe that God cares for them if they see that *I* care for them."

Terri Bannister nodded. "I wish more Christians thought like that. My boss goes to church every Sunday and talks about God all the time, but he always cuts my lunch break short or expects me to work overtime without pay. When I mention it he acts surprised, but nothing ever changes. If I didn't already know the Lord, I'd have a bad attitude toward God because of him." Several others agreed.

Then Ted Newton revealed that he had declined to purchase another year's programming of "Lexa."

"I went through a list of Lexa's shows this past year, and it made me sick. She did interviews like, 'Mothers and Daughters Who Share the Same Lover' and 'Men Who've Killed Their Wives—and Gone Free.' 'Lexa' is one of our most popular daytime shows, but I can't justify it any longer. We're replacing it with a new interactive talk show, 'On Call,' that'll have a changing panel of child psychologists, marriage counselors, drug and alcohol addiction experts, and so forth. They'll take calls and answer questions, then use a computerized list of free counseling services to refer viewers to local help."

"How do you think most people will react to the change?" asked Jason Clark.

"At first, probably like the president of the Broadcast Division," Ted said wryly. "He thought I was crazy. But after I showed him some demographic studies of who our viewers are and surveys showing they're asking for more 'family fare,' he finally agreed to try it. If it doesn't work, though—" Ted raised one dark eyebrow and shrugged. "He's taking a big risk on my word."

A few others shared their experiences at home or on the job and received support and encouragement in turn. When they finally adjourned after silent prayer, many in the group seemed reluctant to leave.

That night, Michael and Sharon stayed up late talking about what they had seen and heard that day. Sharon had spent almost an hour after the evening service talking with Jenny Paige.

"I've never really had the chance before to get to know her," she told Michael, "but she's really serious about this pledge. Did you know that she's the one who just bought the old Jeffers Building downtown?"

"No, but it doesn't surprise me. She and her son own half the commercial property in Ashton's south side."

Sharon looked thoughtful. "She said she was having a hard time deciding what Jesus would do in her place. He never had money or owned property, so the Bible doesn't give her a direct example to follow. She asked us to pray with her about that." She hesitated. "She also asked us to pray for Roger. He hasn't come to either of the pledge meetings, has he?"

"No, and I don't think he's going to. To tell the truth, I think he just comes to church out of habit or maybe to establish business contacts. He's got a pretty wild reputation, the typical 'too much, too soon' scenario. I wouldn't be surprised if he's into some pretty exotic 'recreational' drugs." He added thoughtfully, "I wonder if things would've been different if his father hadn't died when he did. Fourteen is a tough age to be left fatherless."

Before bed, they kneeled together to pray for Jenny, Roger, and many of the others. For the first time in years they both felt connected, closely linked to the lives, joys, and sorrows of their First Church "family."

6

Cliff Bright perched uncomfortably on the kitchen barstool in his posh north Ashton home, drinking coffee and pretending to read the morning paper. The small color television nestled on the counter beneath the polished oak spice cabinets was tuned to Channel 5 News. Although it was barely 8:30 that Monday morning, there had already been a three-car accident on the freeway and a domestic shooting on the south side which left two people dead.

Elizabeth walked in and set her coffee cup down by the sink with unnecessary force. When Cliff flinched, she whirled on him.

"So you're going ahead anyway?" she demanded, her eyes hard behind her glasses. "You're going to ignore my feelings about this silly pledge business and go along with those religious fanatics at First Church? I can't believe it. I just can't believe it!"

"Liz, it's not like that at all," he protested. "I told you; there were about a hundred people there. Even Jenny Paige took the pledge, and *she's* sure no religious fanatic. It's just—it's just something I feel like I should do."

When she didn't respond, Cliff added with unaccustomed firmness, "I'm sorry you're upset. But I already took the pledge, and I'm not going to back out now."

The Brights, to most casual observers, appeared to live an almost storybook existence. They had married straight out of college, when Cliff was a handsome, easygoing accountant and Elizabeth was a popular and cheerful beauty queen. For a wedding present Elizabeth's father, owner of a successful grocery chain in the Southwest, had set Cliff up in his own business by buying him a small corner grocery store in Ashton.

"With a lot of hard work, you'll build this one store into a whole string of stores," he'd told his young son-in-law. "That's how I started, and look at me now!" Elizabeth was thrilled.

Both father and daughter failed to notice that Cliff wasn't interested in owning a string of retail stores. It was a position utterly unsuited to his retiring personality. But what could he do? He thanked his father-in-law and set about the business of being a store owner.

Now, years later, he had succeeded beyond expectations. From that first store, Cliff had built a chain of eighteen thriving Mr. B Food Stores. He was a rich and busy man, and if he ever recalled with regret his early dreams of owning and operating his own small accounting firm, he never mentioned it.

"So what do you plan to do," Elizabeth asked scathingly, "hang pictures of Jesus in all our stores? That'll be great for business."

"No," Cliff said slowly. "I really don't know yet what I'm going to do. I need time to think about it." Elizabeth stormed out of the kitchen, leaving Cliff to stare disconsolately at the paper.

I wonder if it would've been different if we'd been able to have kids, he thought for the millionth time. *Maybe Liz wouldn't be so bitter and pushy. She wanted a baby so badly.*

Three miles away, in the Newtons' brightly wallpapered kitchen, Ted and Kim were bustling around getting ready to leave. Kim worked three mornings a week at Holden Jeweler's in the Ashton Square Mall appraising, cleaning, and repairing jewelry. Her boss had called the previous afternoon to say there were already two rings and a broken bracelet awaiting her attention.

She was rinsing her coffee cup when Ted suddenly stepped up behind her, wrapped her in his arms, and leaned down to quickly kiss her. She laughed, smoothing her wavy, blond hair back into place.

"What's that for?"

"For being such a nice little wife," Ted quipped, then ducked as she slapped playfully at him. "No, really, I'm just glad to be married to you. I feel very lucky."

Kim giggled. "You know, I'm still not sure about this pledge thing at church, but I have to admit you've been a lot nicer to live with lately."

Ted grinned. "In that case, how about meeting me for lunch today? We haven't done that in a long time."

"Sounds good. See you at noon?"

In a modest brick home in the Ashlake subdivision, Terri Bannister had just sent the last of her kids off to the school bus stop. Like so many mornings, Ray had been so rushed that he'd barely taken time to speak to her and the children before he left. It was like he no longer cared that he had a family.

Now, with just fifteen minutes to spare before she had to leave for work, she sat down at the kitchen table and bowed her head.

"Father," she said quietly, "please guide me today in Your ways. And please, Lord, help Ray come to know You."

In an attractively furnished off-campus apartment, Rachel Wingate was just getting up, squinting against the bright sunlight shafting in through her bedroom window. Spring break was over, time once again to hit the books. Her first class started at ten o'clock. Pushing her heavy auburn hair back from her face, she walked, yawning, to the kitchen, and put a cup of water in the microwave. While she waited, she inserted a disc into the CD player in the living room. She liked starting the morning out with music.

A few minutes later, as she sipped hot tea, she wondered—again—how Hallie Collier was doing. It was odd how, in just five short days, the child had become such an important part of her life. The apartment had seemed empty ever since the little girl left for Arizona with her grandparents.

Rachel was momentarily startled when the wall phone rang loudly a few feet away. Still holding her tea, she picked up the receiver.

It was Jason. "Hi, beautiful," he said. "What're you doing?"

Rachel realized that, because of her thoughts, she'd been half expecting it to be the Andersons, Hallie's grandparents. Unfairly, she found Jason's smooth voice suddenly irritating.

"Waking up," she said shortly. "Look, Jason, I've got class this morning, and I'm running a little behind. Can I call you later?"

"Sure. Talk to you then."

Rachel hung up, a little confused by her feelings. She and Jason had been dating steadily for over a year, and lately they'd started talking seriously of marriage. They both loved music and dancing, and there was no question that they found each other attractive. Everyone said they were perfect for each other. *So what's my problem?* Rachel wondered. *Just because he griped about my keeping Hallie is no reason to feel this way. It just bothered me that he kept making snide comments about her being black.*

Still musing, she got dressed and went into the bathroom to put on her makeup. It was then that she spotted the yellow note she'd stuck on the mirror the night before: What Would Jesus Do? *Maybe that's it,* Rachel thought. *Jason took the pledge with me, but it doesn't seem to have meant nearly as much to him. That really bothers me.*

Cheryl Powell looked out her kitchen window, admiring the new green leaves on the towering maple tree in the backyard. She loved the ranch-style home she and Alex had saved for and had built on five wooded acres.

After seeing Alex off several hours earlier, she had enjoyed a few minutes of peace and quiet before her one-year-old granddaughter arrived. She baby-sat little Cara from 7:00 a.m. until noon every day while her daughter worked part time as a nurse's aide.

Now, with the baby contentedly playing with blocks on the living room floor, Cheryl settled down on the couch and opened her Bible. She read for a few minutes, then bowed her head.

Please let Your Spirit lead me today, she prayed. *And show Alex how to be Your representative at the airport.*

At a graceful mansion on Harmony Creek, Jenny Paige paused to pray before she left for her office. . . . Daniel Marshall kneeled in his study to ask for guidance that day at Lincoln Christian College. . . . Dr. West, preparing for an early surgery, silently committed both herself and her patient to the great Physician. . . . Across the city, in various ways, those touched by the First Church pledge prepared for a new day and week of faithfully following in Jesus' steps.

7

MICHAEL MAXWELL ROSE FROM HIS KNEES, THEN slowly walked over to the window. The sky was bright and cloudless.

In the distance, an airplane began its approach toward Vickers Field. Michael saw it sparkle as it circled downward and caught the morning's sunlight. It made him think of Alex Powell. *I still don't know what I'm going to say out there at the Bible study tomorrow morning,* he thought. *I wish I knew more about the problems those people face.*

He'd spent most of the morning praying about that and many other things. His path, in so many ways, was unclear. He needed a concrete plan, some definite course of action for his pastorate of First Church.

With sudden determination, he went back to his desk, turned on his computer, and typed in a centered heading: Things Jesus Probably Would Do as Pastor of First Church. At first all his conflicting ideas made it difficult to sort out his thoughts. But finally he began:

1. He would preach fearlessly against hypocrisy, even if it offended powerful people in His congregation.

2. He would, without hesitation, befriend people of all kinds, disregarding His "image" and not considering Himself above them in any way.

3. He would make sure that all church advertising glorified God instead of people or institutions.

Michael paused, aware of his hesitation to go on. The first three items already meant, for him, some fairly radical changes. But as he'd prayed, he had become increasingly convinced that he needed to ask himself some hard questions—and face the answers.

He continued:

4. He would live in a simple manner, without needless luxury on one hand or undue asceticism on the other.

5. He would work tirelessly to reach and restore those entangled in drug and alcohol abuse and other worldly traps.

6. He would give up the summer trip to Italy and use the money for something less self-indulgent.

He was so absorbed in his thoughts that at first he didn't hear Sharon saying, "Michael? Someone is here to see you."

Behind her stood a sharply-dressed young man who looked vaguely familiar. Michael shook his hand and asked him to be seated. "I don't want to take up too much of your time, Reverend," the man said, "but my partner and I had heard about your church band, and on Sunday we came to hear it for ourselves. It was absolutely incredible!"

Surprised at Michael's lack of response, he continued, "Anyway, I'm here because our company, V. C. Productions, has been looking everywhere for a female singer to play a supporting role in a movie we'll be shooting in Chicago. Your female vocalist—Rachel Wingate, is it?—looks like she'd be perfect."

"What kind of movie is it?" Michael asked slowly.

"It's fantastic, a psychological thriller about a young man with multiple personalities. We'd like to audition Rachel for the role of his girlfriend, a nightclub singer. This guy ends up killing both his parents and almost killing her."

Michael felt sick. "Look, I'll give your card to Ms. Wingate, but I don't know if she'll be interested. If she wants to talk to you, she'll call you back direct. Okay?"

"Fine, fine. But I'll need to hear from her by next week, one way or the other. There's a lot of money involved and plenty of other women who'd kill for a part like this."

After the man left, Maxwell stared unseeingly at the business card in his hand, then went back to his knees. For the next hour he interceded on Rachel's behalf, knowing that the young singer would soon face a difficult decision which could easily change the entire course of her life.

It was a rainy Thursday morning in downtown Ashton. Cliff Bright sat in his sixth floor office at the Ashton Towers going over the previous day's sales reports from his stores. He made notes on a few and set them aside.

A slow and careful thinker, Bright had spent the last three days considering how to apply practically his pledge to ask, "What would Jesus do?" Although some matters still weren't clear, one thing he'd quickly determined—the soft porn magazines stocked in his stores would have to go.

He buzzed his secretary. "Rebecca? Can you come in here please?"

After dictating a company-wide memo ordering that effective immediately all pornographic magazines should be pulled from the shelves, he returned to his scrutiny of the sales reports.

Most of the stores were thriving, but there were one or two serious problems. Store #16 had a continuing pattern of inventory shortage, most likely due to either shoplifting or employee theft. Unfortunately, it was an all-too-common problem. *I'll put security on it,* he thought. *If we don't stop the problem, I'll have to bring in a new manager.*

Another troubled store was #12. Bright noted that sales had dropped over 25 percent in the last six weeks. The accounting department had also attached a note saying that several customers had called to complain that the manager, Connie Garza, had snapped at them.

Bright frowned. Connie had always been one of his best managers: bright, cheerful, popular with customers. It didn't sound like her. He made a note to pay a visit that afternoon to her store.

At WFBB-TV, Ted Newton was dealing with a different kind of problem. Seated across from his desk were two well-dressed salesmen from Adray Brothers, a major distributor of syndicated programming. They were pushing hard to convince him to buy a package of three shows.

One salesman leaned forward in his chair with an earnest look. "I'm really trying to do you a favor here, Mr. Newton. We've already got a strong bid on this package from another station, but I'd like to see you get it. What do you say?"

Ted studied him for a moment, then replied with steel in his voice, "I already told you I'd take the children's science program and 'Movie Reviewers,' but I definitely don't want 'Exposé.' You know as well as I do that tying programs together like that is illegal."

The salesman looked offended. "Look, Mr. Newton, business is business, and anyway, it's no secret that the top shows are only available in packages."

Ted didn't immediately reply. It was true, of course, and in the past he had often bought packages in order to get what he wanted. But now . . .

He abruptly stood up and faced the startled men.

"Then I guess that ends our conversation, gentlemen. I won't participate in unethical practices, and if this is the only way you'll deal with me, you won't be selling to this station anymore at all. I'll see you to the door."

On the way back to his office, Ted wondered grimly how much of an impact the loss of "Movie Reviewers" and "Kid Whiz" would have on Channel 5. He would have to quickly find replacements to run in several sensitive time slots.

But it was the right thing to do, he thought. *Going along with an underhanded deal would make me just as guilty as them.*

His thoughts were interrupted by a tap on the door. Keith Walton entered the office with a broad smile.

"Have you heard the news yet about yesterday's 'Wednesday's Child' show?" he asked.

"No. What happened?"

"We just got a call a few minutes ago from a supervisor with the Child Protective Services. You know the five children who were featured? Since we aired the show, CPS has had over *twenty* calls from families interested in adopting them! She asked if there was any way we would consider running a weekly 'Wednesday's Child' program to help some of the other children find homes."

The news instantly dispelled Ted's earlier gloom. "That's fantastic!" he exclaimed. "What do you think about the idea, Keith?"

The program director grinned sheepishly. "I know I gave you a hard time about it last week, but the more I thought about it, the more convinced I was that you were right. I think we ought to try a weekly show, at least as an experiment."

Keith paused. "Oh, and Ted—," he said, "I want you to know that what you said about your pledge and everything has really made me start thinking. I respect the stand you took." The two men shook hands, grinning, aware of a new bond between them.

Despite the gray drizzle falling steadily on Vickers Field, Alex Powell was having a great day. Sixteen employees had shown up for this morning's Bible study in the break room with Pastor Maxwell. He'd been a little surprised at how quickly the mostly black work crews had accepted the affluent white minister, but his eagerness to learn more about the problems they faced seemed to smooth the way for him to share the gospel.

And the break room looked terrific. The gloomy green walls had been painted a cheerful yellow and the stained ceiling tiles replaced. New tables and chairs had been installed atop gleaming new linoleum, and framed photographs of vintage airplanes graced the walls. The one broken soda machine had been replaced with four snack vending machines, along with a coffeepot, a small refrigerator, and a microwave.

Alex had just returned from lunch. He was in his office reviewing his latest "to do" list on the computer when Corey Snyder, one of five operations officers at the airport, politely knocked on the open door. He had attended the Bible study that morning.

"Alex?" he said. "Can I talk to you for a minute?"

Powell swiveled away from the computer and motioned for him to enter. Snyder dragged a straight chair closer to the desk and sat down.

"You said this morning that if anyone had any ideas about how to improve working conditions around here to tell you about it. I ate lunch in the break room with a bunch of the guys from the electrical shop, and they came up with some good suggestions. Do you have time to listen?"

"Just let me get something to write on." Powell fished out a legal pad from an untidy stack of papers on his desk, pulled a pen from his drawer, then said, "Okay, I'm ready."

"First of all, fixing up the break room was a great idea. When I was down there today there must have been fifteen or twenty people in there eating, and they all think you're a hero." Snyder grinned. "They're talking about hanging your picture in a place of honor over the microwave."

Powell chuckled, flattered. "That would make them all lose their appetites. I think they'd better stick with airplanes."

Snyder smiled. "Anyway, several of the older guys brought up the fact that they'd like to learn to use the computers in their departments instead of always having to depend on the younger workers. They wondered if some kind of in-house training program might be possible."

Powell was impressed. "I don't know why not. I actually think it's a great idea, and that's a skill they could transfer to other jobs too. I'll see what I can do." He made a note on the pad.

"Several others mentioned that in the city their same jobs involve both more responsibility and more money. They wondered if, at some point, they could have their positions redefined to get them more personally involved in how the airport is run. A lot of them have worked here for years, and they feel they could be used more efficiently—and paid more fairly."

Powell nodded slowly. "That sounds reasonable. You know, I wonder—what do you think about setting up some kind of monthly brainstorming session where employees can share ideas like this directly with management?"

"I think it would work. There are a lot of good people here who'd like to feel they can make a difference. Their satisfaction with their jobs would definitely go up if they felt someone was seriously listening to them."

"That's understandable. Thanks for taking the time, Corey. I'll see what I can do about these things."

After the operations officer left, Alex studied the notes he'd made on the legal pad. The effect of the pledge he'd taken was already spreading to an ever-widening group of people, some whose names he didn't even know. The realization left him both grateful and excited.

Cliff Bright eased his bulk with some difficulty from behind the steering wheel of his expensive car, now parked in front of Store #12. Through the glass storefront he could see Connie Garza waiting on a customer, a heavyset man in construction clothes.

When Cliff opened the door, an electronic chime sounded. Garza looked up, her eyes widening when she saw it was "Mr. B" himself.

He tried to ease her discomfort with a friendly smile, but the strain in her face was unmistakable. What had happened to etch those anxious lines into the bubbly young store manager's face?

"I just dropped by to check in with you, Connie," Bright said casually. "How's everything going?"

"Okay I guess, Mr. Bright," she replied with a soft Hispanic accent. When she turned to wait on another customer, Bright studied her profile. Although her thick dark hair was pulled neatly back into a ponytail, her uniform shirt had several stains. One button was missing, clumsily replaced with a safety pin. Her name tag was askew.

The store was also in less than immaculate condition. The floor needed sweeping, and many of the shelves were poorly stocked and in disarray. The glass doors of the refrigerated section were thickly fingerprinted.

When the store was empty again, Cliff said gently, "Connie, I think we need to talk."

To his dismay, her eyes instantly brimmed with tears. She sank onto the tall stool behind the counter and covered her face with both hands. Cliff watched helplessly as her shoulders began to shake with silent sobs.

Just then the bell sounded announcing the entrance of a customer. Cliff quickly moved behind the counter and spoke to the shaken manager. "Connie, go to the back and relax for a few minutes. I'll watch the counter."

The next time the store emptied, Bright hand-lettered a Closed for One Hour sign and taped it to the front door. Then he went back to the employee area where Garza waited.

She looked up. "I'm sorry, Mr. Bright," she said desperately. "I don't usually act like this; I really don't. It's just—"

Cliff held both palms up in a calming gesture. "It's okay. Let's just talk for a few minutes, all right?"

From the moment he'd seen the store's condition, Bright had realized the logical solution was to replace Garza. Although firing managers was one of his least favorite tasks, it was often necessary. He normally didn't hesitate.

But now, seeing Connie's condition, he didn't want to act hastily. Part of it was because of her past work record, but another part was due, oddly enough, to Brenda Collier. After her death, Bright had quietly inquired to see if the convenience store that had fired her when she got sick was one of his. As it turned out, it wasn't—but it easily could have been.

"Has something been going on with your family, Connie?" he asked. "You don't seem your usual self."

She didn't meet his eyes. "Yes, sir," she said. "Four months ago, my husband started having bad coughing fits. He's smoked since he was fourteen so he's always coughed a lot, but when he started coughing up blood I made him go to the doctor. They sent him in for a chest X-ray—he has lung cancer."

Cliff shook his head in sympathy but didn't say anything.

She went on, "He went in for surgery three weeks ago, and they took out part of one lung. He's been going through chemotherapy since then, but we don't really know how much good it's doing. He can't work, and he's sick all the time. It's taken every dime just to meet our part of the insurance."

She finally met Bright's eyes. "I know I've been letting things here slip," she said pleadingly. "I'll try to do better. I really will. I—I don't know what I'd do if I lost my job on top of everything else right now."

Bright quickly put her mind at ease. "You're not going to lose your job, Connie. You've been a good manager for a long time, and I know you'll work through this. What can I do to help you?"

Unexpectedly, the young manager once again burst into tears. "I don't know what to say," she sobbed in relief. "I'm so tired and irritable these days, and I barely have enough energy to get up in the morning, much less to stock shelves. I know my sales have gone down."

"Would it help if I temporarily assigned an extra clerk here to help you get everything back in order?"

"Yes, I think it would. Could you do that?"

Bright smiled. "I'm the boss, remember? I can do whatever I want." His words brought a faint smile to the harried manager's face.

Before he left, Bright called and arranged for a clerk to be transferred from one of the other stores to #12. He also invited Connie to church the following Sunday. "You need to be around people who care about you and your husband," he told her. "It can make a big difference to know you're not facing it all alone." She said she would try to come.

Cliff found himself humming as he drove back to his office. *Maybe,* he thought, *having to run a chain of convenience stores isn't so bad after all.*

8

Rachel Wingate stared incredulously at Pastor Maxwell. Earlier, when she received the message from him requesting that she drop by the church office, she'd gone expecting to hear about a change in the music program for Sunday. Instead, Michael told her of the offer from V. C. Productions.

"You mean they actually want to give me a part where I'd get to sing?" she asked excitedly. "I can't believe it!"

Maxwell handed her the man's business card, then looked at her steadily. "He'll explain about the movie and part when you call him. But Rachel, why don't we pray about it now and ask for the Holy Spirit's guidance?" She quickly agreed.

Back at home, Rachel dialed the number for V. C. Productions and was soon put through to Mark Downs, one of the producers. He quickly described the movie, *Secret Rage*, and her part as a nightclub singer.

"This is a large role for a newcomer," he said, "but my partner and I heard you sing at First Church, and we think you'll be perfect. Can you come to our Chicago office Monday morning to read for us?"

"I'd love to," Rachel said, "but I'd like to ask a few questions first. Will this role require me—" she paused, then plunged on in embarrassment—"will it require me to curse or to appear in any—in any compromising scenes?"

Downs laughed. "Honey, give me a break. For God's sake, you'll be a *nightclub singer!* You'll have to swear, of course, and there's one love scene. But you don't have to get naked or anything; you can wear a flesh-colored body suit if you want. We'll manage the rest with camera angles."

Rachel was silent for a moment. "I'd like to have time to think this over. Can I call you back on Monday?"

Downs was irritated. "Sure, sure, honey. But I hope you have better sense than to let some moralistic ideas keep you from the chance of a lifetime. Talk to you then."

The phone clicked in Rachel's ear. Chewing her lip, she slowly replaced the receiver. She thought for a moment, then picked up the phone again and called Jason.

A few minutes later her doorbell rang. As always, Rachel was struck by Jason's physical presence, his muscular physique, and clear blue eyes. He took her in his arms briefly, then she invited him to sit down.

She quickly explained the offer from V. C. Productions. She told him everything, including the amount of money involved and the role requirements. Then she looked him in the face.

"What do you think I should do, Jason? It's a great opportunity, but I'm still not sure about it, especially in view of our First Church pledge. I mean, it's not *all* that bad, and I guess it might actually lead to other roles where I could be more selective, but still—"

Jason, excited, waved aside her concerns. "Hey, you can't expect your first role to be just what you want. But later on, who knows? You might be able to do a lot of good once you're established in the industry. Maybe this is God's plan for you."

His soothing words and reassurances slowly erased the troubled lines on Rachel's forehead. "Maybe you're right," she said, her eyes suddenly sparkling. "Oh, Jason, can you believe it? I'm going to be a *movie star!*"

It was only later, after he left, that she walked into her bathroom to see the small yellow note stuck on the mirror: What Would Jesus Do?

The simple words sent a wave of doubt washing over her again, leaving her torn and agitated. Irritated, she jerked the note off and crumpled it in her hand—then stood frozen, staring at her image in the mirror. Slowly, tears welled in her eyes and spilled down her cheeks.

What am I doing? she thought. Carefully smoothing the note, she stuck it back on the mirror, then went into her bedroom and sank to her knees on the white carpet.

Father, she prayed, *You know how much I'd like to do a movie. But if that's not what You want for me, I'll obey and follow You.*

At about that same time, Alex Powell was walking back into his office with a fresh cup of coffee, hoping to get some paperwork done. He had just set the cup down next to his computer when the phone rang.

"Alex?" said Chuck Finley. "Do you have a minute to talk about Jet-Rep?" Jet-Rep was an aircraft repair and maintenance company that was building a large new facility at Vickers Field.

"Sure. What's the problem?"

"No problem, really. We just need to speed things up. When do you think we'll get the board's approval for the security system we need?"

Alex grinned into the receiver. "You know how fast they move, Chuck. It could be next week, or it could be three weeks from now. Is there a rush?"

There was a slight pause. "Well," Finley said casually, "you know we've already got the runway extension under construction, and by next week the new building will be far enough along for us to start installing the security system. We can't afford any delays on this project."

Alex frowned, puzzled. "How can it possibly be that far along already? We only signed the agreement with Jet-Rep three months ago."

There was another significant pause. Four months before, when Jet-Rep had approached the airport about building a new facility on its grounds, it had caused a great deal of excitement. A lease agreement with the aircraft repair company would not only benefit the airport, it would also create almost five hundred new jobs in the area.

There was only one major problem: Vickers' runways weren't sufficient to handle the larger commercial aircraft Jet-Rep maintained and serviced. Although the location was ideal, Jet-Rep was considering two other regional airports as well.

"Alex," Finley finally said. "The only way we got Jet-Rep to commit to the lease agreement was by promising to have the facility *and* a runway extension finished in six months."

Alex was stunned. "How could you promise them that? It sometimes takes the board that long just to *approve* a big contract like that!"

"We didn't go through the board." Finley sighed. "Look, I know you're not going to like this, but going through normal channels would've made it impossible. Stokes and I talked to the director about it, and we found a way around all the red tape. Instead of presenting it as one major contract and going through the normal bidding and approval process, we divided it up into a number of smaller contracts, all under the per-item cost limits. We've had construction crews out there working around the clock for weeks."

Alex gripped the phone receiver tightly, a sick feeling deep in his stomach. "Did you talk to *any* of the board members about this?"

Finley laughed. "Are you kidding? Most of those guys are political appointees who don't know one end of an airplane from the other. They wouldn't care that it might cost Vickers the lease agreement with Jet-Rep. They'd insist on business as usual."

Now it was Alex's turn to be silent. Vickers Field was regulated by the city of Ashton with rigid standards and procedures for all airport expansion or improvements. What Finley had just described to him was borderline fraud, a deliberate flaunting of the regulatory board's authority.

Why did he have to tell me? he thought. *I'd rather not know anything about it.*

But like it or not, he did know—and he was now faced with a wrenching decision. What, if anything, should he do with his knowledge?

That Saturday, the *Ashton Herald* contained a feature article about Ted Newton. The Child Protective Services worker who had called Channel 5 to report the exciting results of the "Wednesday's Child" broadcast had also called the newspaper, hoping to apply public pressure to the station to air similar programs in the future. A reporter had been dispatched to WFBB-TV. The article started by detailing the happy results of the Wednesday broadcast, then continued:

> According to at least one Channel 5 employee, the decision to preempt the hit talk show "Lexa" in order to air

the "Wednesday's Child" special was made by Ted Newton, president and general manager of WFBB-TV. But apparently it was just one of many controversial decisions Newton has recently made, including dropping "Lexa" entirely for the next season in favor of a "healthier" talk show, "On Call." Newton is also said to be considering dropping several major clothing and perfume advertisers' commercial spots unless they "clean them up."

Why the sudden change? Newton says he "no longer feels comfortable airing shows [he] perceives as damaging to families.

"I hope to see Channel 5 gain a reputation in our community as a leader in responsible programming and reporting," Newton says. "I'd like concerned parents to know that their children can safely watch Channel 5 without being exposed to vulgar shows or commercials, or to movies that subtly undermine their values."

Many people might say that Ted Newton's ideas are unrealistic in this day and age, but after seeing the joy on the faces of the five youngsters tentatively placed for adoption this last week thanks to Channel 5, I'm not so sure.

Only time—and the ratings—will tell.

9

THE AFTER-CHURCH MEETING THAT SUNDAY HAD to be moved out of the lecture room when more than a hundred people showed up.

As they filed back into the sanctuary they'd just left, there seemed to be an unusual amount of excitement in the air. Rachel Wingate, trailed by a sulky Jason Clark, was talking animatedly with Jenny Paige. A small group was clustered around Ted Newton talking to him about the *Herald* article. Kim, at his side, looked positively radiant.

Alex and Cheryl Powell, on the other hand, were abnormally quiet. Before the service that morning, Alex had drawn Michael aside and asked to speak with him privately after the meeting. The minister had quickly agreed.

After opening with prayer, Michael asked if anyone wanted to share a testimony. Several people laughed when Ted immediately jumped to his feet.

"Sorry, but I'm about to burst," he said with a sheepish grin. "This has been an incredible week. I don't know how many of you saw the 'Wednesday's Child' special we ran a few days ago, but it was about five 'hard to place' children in the area who needed adoptive homes. You might have already read it in the *Ashton Herald*, but after our show, Child Protective Services got calls from more than twenty couples interested in adopting!

"The thing is, I almost didn't allow the show to air. If it weren't for the pledge I'd taken here, 'Lexa' would've run like usual—and five kids would still be homeless."

As he sat back down there was a spontaneous burst of applause, not for Ted but for the Lord who had led him so faithfully. Then Jenny Paige stood up, ignoring an attempt by Rachel Wingate to stop her.

"Rachel's not going to tell you about this, so I'm going to instead," she said briskly. "This last week, a production company offered her a part as a nightclub singer in a television movie being filmed in Chicago. The part involved a lot of money, but it also involved a sex scene and a fair amount of cursing.

"But in keeping with her pledge, Rachel asked herself honestly what Jesus would do—then did it."

Jenny looked down at the young woman fondly. "She turned down the offer, and I, for one, am extremely proud of her."

A murmur of agreement ran through the crowd.

An elderly man leaned forward to pat Rachel's shoulder. "Young lady," he said softly, "God will give you something a hundred times better than what you gave up; you wait and see." She smiled wanly, the pain of the decision still evident on her face.

Several people were surprised when Cliff Bright spoke up after a moment. Although he and Elizabeth had been First Church members for more than six years, few people knew them well. Cliff usually seemed withdrawn and a little sad. Now, though, his round face was positively beaming.

"I had an interesting week," he said. "I began my pledge later than some of you, so I'm really just getting started.

"There are lots of things I haven't thought through yet, but one thing I quickly decided is that Jesus wouldn't sell or distribute 'girlie' magazines in any store He owned. As of several days ago, none of my stores carry them anymore."

This time there was no hesitation; everyone cheered. "You did the right thing," Terri Bannister told him. "I've always hated taking my kids into convenience stores because of that." Others also chimed in to express their support and encouragement.

But Cliff wasn't finished. "What's really exciting, though, is that I saw one of my store managers here in church this morning. In all the years I've thought of myself as a 'Christian employer,' I've never even considered inviting an employee to church. Taking this pledge is changing my whole attitude toward them, and even toward the job itself."

Several other stories were shared, then the group prayed together, this time taking turns praying for one another. An intense feeling of love swept over the room as the Spirit once again demonstrated His presence, bringing a strong sense of family to those gathered in Jesus' name.

When the meeting was finally dismissed, Alex and Cheryl Powell lingered behind in the quiet sanctuary. "Come on back to my office," Michael told them.

The three talked long and earnestly, then solemnly knelt together to seek God's face. If anyone had chanced to look into the church office at that moment, they might have caught a glimpse of an intense spiritual battle being waged.

Two weeks later, the *Ashton Herald* carried another front-page story about a First Church member.

ASHTON—Yesterday, long-time Vickers Field Operations Manager Alex Powell turned in his resignation after appearing before the airport regulatory board to expose unethical contract practices used in recent new construction on airport property. His revelations have caused a formal investigation to be launched into the multi-million-dollar Jet-Rep project.

In a statement televised last night on Channel 5, WFBB-TV, Powell, visibly shaken, expressed deep regret over having to expose the scandal at the airport where he's worked for almost fifteen years, but said his silence would have made him as "morally responsible" as those who participated in the fraudulent practices. Although he wasn't required to resign, he said he felt it best since he will be called to testify against several highly placed airport officials, including his own direct superior, the director of aviation.

He offered his full support to Richard Olds, the new operations manager at Vickers Field.

10

MICHAEL AND SHARON ATE A QUIET BREAKFAST, sobered by the morning paper's announcement of Alex Powell's resignation.

"I need to go see him tonight," Michael said. "He did this because of his pledge. He told me weeks ago about this whole situation, and we prayed together for guidance. I guess he got his answer."

Sharon looked up, troubled. "The paper says this will probably kill the Jet-Rep project and cause over five hundred jobs that were coming into Ashton to be moved to Norville. Michael, do you really think Jesus would've done that?"

He considered. "I think," he said thoughtfully, "that, given the same circumstances, He probably would. But the point is, Alex believes that's what He would do, and it's his responsibility to follow through with it."

He added, "It was no easy decision for him, Sharon. In less than a year he would have been eligible for full retirement benefits. Now his and Cheryl's future looks pretty uncertain.

They're still making payments on their new house, you know."

Although Powell's action had created a sensation in Ashton, other strange events involving First Church members had also drawn a lot of attention. The reforms Cliff Bright had made in his stores had inspired many favorable comments, as had Ted Newton's ongoing changes at Channel 5. All through the city—in homes, businesses, and social circles—people were starting to ask, "What's getting into these Christians?"

One instantly noticeable change was in the First Church billboard along the highway.

Soon after Michael had written his list of things Jesus might do as pastor of First Church, he had called the deacons together to talk about the church advertising. Several of them were astonished at the abrupt turnaround in the minister's attitude, but they agreed to modify the mail-out fliers, and also to have the billboard repainted. Michael's photograph was replaced with a picture of a rough-hewn wooden cross, and the billboard now read:

If Anyone Would Come After Me,
He Must Deny Himself and Take Up His Cross
And Follow Me.
Matthew 16:24

Although many both in and out of the church welcomed the changes, there were a few who found the harsh cross image distasteful. One was Martha Robinson, the church treasurer.

"I don't know what Pastor Maxwell is thinking," she complained to members of the building committee. "First this pledge thing, and now shoving a *cross* in people's faces—as if that will make them want to join our church! And I'll tell you another thing; our attendance *and* collections have steadily gone down over the last six weeks. If he keeps this up, he's going to run this church into the ground."

Michael heard about the conversation when one of the older building committee members came to him, troubled about the growing division in the church.

"Pastor, I've been attending First Church since it began over thiry-five years ago, and in that time I've outlasted six preachers," he said. "Each time, it started like this, with little complaints and grumblings. I wouldn't want to see that happen to you."

Michael smiled. "I'm afraid I've been so busy I haven't even noticed, but I appreciate your concern. I'm not going to change what I'm doing, though, because I honestly believe it's what Jesus would do."

That evening Michael went out to the Powell's house to talk and pray with them. After he got home, he sank wearily into a chair.

"Alex and Cheryl are both really broken up over this, Sharon," he said. "Not only over Alex's job, but because he was just starting to see some really good things happen out there at Vickers. He's hoping that Richard Olds, the man who's replacing him, will continue a lot of the things he started."

Sharon moved behind him and began to gently massage his neck and shoulders as he continued. "I'll call Cheryl in the morning. She probably needs some moral support about now, too."

She moved around to perch on the arm of his chair, suddenly aware of several new lines in Michael's face. Less than two months into his pledge, he was already starting to show the physical strain of bearing the burdens of those who, with him, had promised to "take up their crosses" and follow Christ.

Letters to the Editor of the *Ashton Herald*:

Dear Sir:

Regarding the recent action of Alex Powell, former operations manager at Vickers Field Regional Airport, I'd like to say that I'm astonished and outraged that, for the sake of his rather vague "principles" over a minor point, he would throw away five hundred new jobs for Ashton.

Harry Chandler, Director
Ashton Community Affairs Center

To the Editor:

Since I'm one of the unemployed people who had hoped to be hired at Jet-Rep, I'd like to say, "Thanks a lot, Mr. Powell! Are you going to bring food to my house now for my family?"

Rick Morrow

Dear Editor:

Just who does Alex Powell think he is, anyway? I personally applaud the community-minded people at Vickers Field who had the courage to risk sidestepping the bureaucratic "procedure" (i.e., red tape) in order to bring additional jobs and money into Ashton.

Councilman Don Essenpreis
City Council District #2

Dear Sir:

Instead of going straight to the media, why didn't Mr. Powell approach the airport director or other airport officials to see if the problem could be quietly resolved without jeopardizing the Jet-Rep project? It's apparent by his actions that Mr. Powell was more interested in publicity and raising a scandal than in the welfare of our community.

Jonathan Spire

To the Editor:

We the undersigned would like to publicly state our support for Alex Powell with regard to his recent dealings with Vickers Field. Many of us have worked with him for over ten years and know him as a man of absolute honesty and integrity. We will miss him.

Custodial and Maintenance Crew Members,
Vickers Field Airport—
Joe Crain, Carlos Ramirez, Eric Seidler, Kevin Robinson, John Harney, Maggie Whitehead, Sue Setley, Kathy Fieler, David Smith Maria Langer, Roger Franz, Scott Henderson, Richard Collins, Gary Sledge, Belinda Buckingham

---

Private letter from Pastor Maxwell:

Dear Alex and Cheryl,

I can only imagine the pain you both must be experiencing over this whole situation and the deep sense of loss Alex, especially, must feel. I can't begin to tell you how much I admire and appreciate your faithfulness in keeping your pledge to follow Jesus at all costs.

I deeply respect your continued refusal to answer the repeated attacks in the newspaper—especially since your accusers have so many wrong facts. If they only realized how you tried to "quietly resolve" the problem with the director or how much you lost by going public! I believe you're taking the higher road, as Jesus did:

"When they hurled their insults at him, he did not retaliate; when he suffered, he made no threats. Instead, he entrusted himself to him who judges justly" (1 Pet. 2:23).

As your pastor, I can only say "thank you" for your faithfulness, and promise that my thoughts and prayers will be with you as you walk through this dark time.

Pastor Michael Maxwell

11

The weeks that followed saw several interesting developments. One was the growing friendship between Rachel Wingate and Jenny Paige.

Ever since the Sunday when Rachel talked to the older woman about the V. C. Productions offer, the two had spoken regularly. They met twice in the city for lunch, then Jenny invited Rachel home for dinner. Rachel was overwhelmed by her first glimpse inside the Paige mansion.

"I can't believe this!" she breathed, staring from the graceful winding staircase to the small fountain near the entryway. The floor was gleaming marble, scattered with costly Oriental rugs. A heavy crystal chandelier was suspended from the raised ceiling in the dining room to the left.

Jenny smiled at her reaction. "Not exactly cozy, is it? My husband had this built during his high-roller days, and I hated to sell it after he passed away. It has one advantage, though; if I get upset with Roger, there's enough room here for him to stay out of my way."

Rachel grinned. "Where is Roger, anyway? I haven't seen much of him lately."

"He'll be here for dinner. I think he had other plans, but when he heard you were coming he suddenly decided he should spend more time with his dear old mother. Having a young, pretty girl here definitely adds to my charm."

Rachel laughed. "You're not a bit old. I can't even think of you as being my mother's age. You seem so much more—I don't know, alive or something."

Jenny was obviously pleased. "Well, I'm alive enough to be famished. Let's go see if we can hurry dinner along."

They were in the kitchen chatting with the cook when Roger walked in. He stopped short when he saw Rachel.

"Well, hello there!" he said, flashing her a grin. "I didn't know you were already here."

Clad in gym clothes with his brown hair tousled and sweaty, he used the towel around his neck to quickly wipe his face. Although his features were a little too blunt to be called handsome, he'd always been careful about his appearance. He was also acutely aware that, for most girls, his bank account greatly improved his looks.

Rachel hid an amused smile. "We were just scouting for food. Your mom and I have been working up an appetite wandering around this house. It's huge!"

Roger shrugged. "It's no big deal," he said with a smugness that belied his words. "Just a place to live." Reaching into the refrigerator, he drew out a wine cooler, twisted off the lid, and raised it in a mocking toast to his mother and Rachel before taking a long drink. "I guess I'll see you in a few minutes, ladies. I need to grab a quick shower."

Jenny and Rachel had already started eating when Roger came back in, his hair damp but combed. As he slid into a chair across the table, Rachel noticed for the first time how much he resembled Jenny in the strong lines of his face. His keen blue eyes were emphasized by the bright pattern of his shirt.

"So," he said pleasantly, "what brings you out to the Paige Mausoleum?" He served himself generously from a steaming platter of broccoli and ladled some gravy onto his potatoes. "We don't have many non-business visitors these days."

"Actually, your mom and I have been talking business. She was telling me about some of the property Paige, Inc., bought down in the south side a few months ago." Rachel looked at the older woman. "Have you already told him any of this?"

Jenny shook her head. "We were discussing the Jeffers Building, Roger. We came up with an idea that we both like."

The Jeffers Building was an old, run-down four-story structure situated at the heart of the roughest area of Ashton's south side. Long vacant, it had been repeatedly vandalized; most of its windows were broken out and replaced by steel bars. Since it was often used during the winter as a shelter by "street people," the air inside was pungent with the smells of urine and vomit. Drug deals and rape, even murder, were part of daily life in the area.

"The best idea for that eyesore is a bulldozer," Roger said firmly. "Even if we fixed it up, no business would want to locate there."

"That's the point," Rachel said. "There's only one thing it would be just perfect for—a gospel mission!"

Roger paused, fork in hand, to stare from Rachel to his mother. "A *mission?* You mean like a church?"

Jenny nodded. "But not like a regular church. It would be aimed at the street people in the area, and it would go beyond just preaching. There's already a kitchen downstairs that could be refurbished, and the upstairs could be equipped with cots and showers. It would be more like a shelter, a place where people could come in, hear a message of hope, then get a hot meal and a bed. Can you think of a more effective way to get through to them?"

Roger was cynical. "They'd just use the system to get what they want. Most of those people live the way they do because they *want* to, not because they have to. It would be a total waste of time and money."

"I don't think so," Rachel contradicted him. "But even if some of them 'used' the system, it would still serve its purpose for others. Anyway, we're going to talk to Pastor Maxwell about it and see what he thinks."

Roger looked at his mother quizzically, then briefly shifted his gaze to Rachel. What was it in their faces that suddenly seemed so—*vital?*

The atmosphere was tense in the tall Ashton Towers conference room as almost twenty store managers waited nervously for "Mr. B's" arrival. Rumors had run rampant ever since the meeting had been announced.

"I hear he plans to fire us all and replace us with people from his church," one man said. "He's on some Jesus thing where he only wants Christian managers."

"Well, if he tries that he's gonna be sorry," a woman said belligerently. "I'll sue him so fast he won't know what hit him. That's discrimination!" A growing rumble of assent was abruptly cut short when Cliff Bright entered the room and walked to the front. He greeted several managers by name, then called the meeting to order.

"I understand," he began, "that some of you are concerned that I called this meeting to fire everybody." He paused to smile. "Although there've been weeks when that might have sounded tempting, I assure you that's not why you're here."

Several people exchanged relieved glances. The woman who had spoken earlier settled back in her chair. In the front row Connie Garza listened quietly, her dark eyes on Bright's face.

He continued, "Actually, I want to announce some changes that I hope to introduce into the stores over the next few months, and also to get your advice and input about ways we can improve Mr. B's. You know your customers better than I do, and I thought you might have specific ideas about things you might like to see happen in each of your stores."

At his words, several managers nodded and whispered excitedly to each other. Bright waited for the murmur to die down before speaking again.

"You're all aware that, as of several weeks ago, Mr. B Food Stores no longer sell pornographic magazines. Although that decision has cost the company a considerable amount of money, I believe it was the right thing to do. We don't need money earned by selling trash."

Several of the female managers burst into spontaneous applause. Bright, startled but pleased, waited till it died down, then went on.

"The more I've thought about it, though, the more convinced I've become that there are other significant changes that need to be made as well. And frankly, they might end up being even more costly."

At his solemn tone, a worried silence once again descended over the room. What did he have in mind?

"Over these past two weeks I've made it a point to visit each one of your stores—not for the usual reasons—but to get a better feel for how we're serving the community. I must say that it left me with a lot of thinking to do. None of what I'm going to say next is a reflection on any of you. The products in your stores has always been my responsibility, not yours.

But since that's the case, it's now my responsibility to correct some bad decisions I've made in the past.

"First, as your stores sell out of tobacco products, I don't want you to reorder. Too many people today are suffering and dying because of tobacco use, and even though I realize it's perfectly legal, I don't want to be guilty of contributing, even indirectly, to anyone's addiction." His eyes rested briefly on Connie's face.

"Second, I want you to follow the same no-reorder policy with all hard liquor. I don't claim to know a whole lot about alcohol, but it seems to me that the main purpose of buying hard liquor is to get drunk. For the time being, we will continue to carry beer and wine, but any store employee I catch selling to a minor will be instantly dismissed."

The news of those two changes alone was enough to leave the managers wide-eyed, but before it could all sink in, Bright opened the floor to discussion. Connie Garza hesitated, then slipped up her hand. When Bright nodded, she stood up.

"Lots of my customers work at the steel shop down the street," she said. "Several of them have asked me why we don't open a deli at Mr. B so they can buy fresh sandwiches during their lunch break."

Several managers nodded, and Bright jotted the idea down on a notepad. "That's an interesting idea, Connie. I'll check into it. Anyone else?"

"If we're going to talk about opening a deli, why not a bakery too?" suggested one man. "Some of my customers buy the prepackaged donuts for breakfast every morning, but if we had fresh donuts—even a small selection—I'll bet we'd sell out. There isn't a donut shop for miles around."

The other managers, getting into the spirit, talked in low murmurs as Bright noted the man's comments. When he asked for the next suggestion, four people raised their hands.

"This isn't about a new product or anything," a woman said, "but my sister works in a Quik-Mart down in Tennessee, and after she got robbed one night, her boss installed a kind of cage of bulletproof glass around the counter. I don't know about anybody else, but something like that would make me feel a lot safer when I have to work alone late at night." Several others echoed their support of the idea, and Bright wrote it down.

The meeting continued for another hour, with manager after manager standing up to make suggestions. The atmosphere became jovial, with frequent laughter and a growing sense of camaraderie between Bright and his employees. When they were dismissed, many stayed behind to chat with Mr. B. Bright left that afternoon with a light heart. *I've never seen them so fired up about making their stores succeed,* he thought. *If anything will help us weather the rough months ahead, it will be that.*

12

The First Church pledge was now entering its fourth month. The number attending the Sunday after-church meetings had steadily grown, and the regulars, now numbering more than 150, greeted each other with joyful familiarity. The common bond between them made it seem increasingly natural to share their experiences.

The growing success of the meetings, however, had led some of the deacons and other church administrators to complain of "cliquishness" in the church.

"Going to these 'pledge meetings' is getting to be like some kind of status symbol," Martha Robinson had muttered darkly at their last meeting. "If Pastor Maxwell doesn't put a stop to it soon, the Board is going to get some letters calling for his resignation."

"From what I've seen," one deacon said quietly, "a lot of people who've taken the pledge don't stay for the meetings, and some who attend the meetings haven't taken the pledge at all. Have you ever gone to one?"

"No, and I don't plan to, either. Doesn't the Bible say that we're all one body? I think this is just another way for people to be 'holier-than-thou.'"

This Sunday, however, Michael Maxwell noticed that several people were missing from the after-meeting—Jason Clark among them. He had excused himself right after church, citing a last-minute schedule conflict. Michael noticed he had carefully avoided Rachel's appraising look as he left.

Catching sight of the Powells across the room, Michael slowly worked his way in their direction. Alex had just started a new job in neighboring Guilford as an FAA inspector, so it looked like he and Cheryl wouldn't end up suffering too much financially. But the transition had been rough.

"How's everything going?" Michael asked, shaking Alex's hand warmly. "Do you have your new boss trained yet?"

Alex shook his head ruefully. "It's not easy calling a supervisor half my age 'sir'—especially when most of the time he doesn't know what he's talking about. He has a degree, but less than two years' airport experience!" He sighed. "It takes just about everything I've got just to get through each day."

Maxwell patted his shoulder. "Well, it might cheer you up to hear that last week, two men at the Vickers Bible study committed their lives to the Lord and asked to be baptized. The group gets bigger almost every week, and it wouldn't have happened without you, Alex."

Alex brightened. "That's good. That's great! Thanks a lot for letting me know."

After the opening prayer, several people shared testimonies and special prayer requests; then Cliff Bright stood up.

His usually florid face was slightly pale this morning, and he seemed to have lost some weight. Although Elizabeth had never relented in her opposition to his attendance of the First Church after-meetings, he hadn't missed a single one since he had taken the pledge. He had grown especially close to Ted Newton and Daniel Marshall.

Facing the crowd, Bright cleared his throat. "I'm afraid my news isn't as positive as some of the other testimonies this morning," he said slowly. "I put this off for as long as I could, hoping it would eventually take care of itself. But unless something dramatic happens soon, it looks like I'm going to have to close several of my stores."

His announcement left many people shocked. Even those who didn't know the store owner well had come to admire and respect him over the preceding months. His spiritual insight and thoughtful responses had caused many of them to look to him for leadership and advice.

Bright continued, "Most of you remember that soon after taking the pledge I decided to stop selling 'girlie' magazines and to pull all tobacco products and hard liquor from my stores' shelves. I made those decisions after a lot of prayer, believing that they were what Jesus would do in my place.

"I wasn't surprised when the company showed an immediate loss; the magazines were a big money-maker. But over the next few months, the additional losses from tobacco and liquor added up to a total income drop of over *31 percent!* No company can take a loss like that for long and stay in business.

"I called a meeting with all my managers to discuss ways we might be able to compensate for those losses, and they came up with great ideas which I think, in time, could be a great success. I've invested a significant sum of money in adding small delis to five of the stores and bakeries to another six. But the bottom line is, unless we get a major boost in sales over the next six to eight weeks, I'll be forced to make drastic cuts—most likely by closing stores."

He looked around the room. "What I'm most concerned about at this point are my employees. Several of them are in financial straits and couldn't afford to lose their jobs and health insurance. It isn't their fault that I'm no longer giving them the kind of products people obviously want to buy! I'd appreciate it if you'd all pray for me over the upcoming weeks that I'll make the right decisions."

Alex Powell was listening thoughtfully. "Cliff, have you decided yet whether or not you're going to pull beer and wine out of your stores, too? You'd talked about that before." Alex, with his near-shattering experience years before, was opposed to the sale of alcohol in any form.

"I'm not really sure at this point," Cliff said honestly. "I know a lot of Christians believe it's wrong to drink under any circumstances, and I can't argue the fact that alcohol has caused a lot of grief and misery. But from my understanding of the Bible, it's drunkenness that's condemned, not alcohol itself. I'd appreciate it if you'd pray with me about that as well."

After Cliff sat down, there was a moment of silence. Then Kim Newton impulsively stood up and faced the group.

"I don't know about the rest of you," she said, "but I have a lot of respect for what Mr. Bright is doing. Why don't we back him with our purchases as well as with our prayers? If every one of us here today made it a point to shop at Mr. B Food Stores from now on and encouraged our friends and neighbors to shop there, too, couldn't we make a difference? I bet lots of people would be willing to go out of their way if they realized what was happening."

Ted, surprised at his wife's spirited outburst, enthusiastically voiced his agreement. He was quickly joined by all the others.

Michael Maxwell stood up. "That's a great idea, Kim. The church can help, too, by buying the donuts and coffee for our fellowship breakfasts there from now on." Cliff listened in astonishment, overwhelmed by their promises of support.

Then Jenny Paige spoke up. "Cliff," she said briskly, "I can't help but think that, with the Christian community behind you, things will turn around quickly. But will you make sure to let us know how things are going, whether it's good news or bad?" Cliff nodded in agreement.

Jenny smiled. "Well," she said, "while I'm already talking I guess I might as well share some other news. For the past few weeks, Rachel Wingate and I have been working on an idea for an inner-city outreach down on the south side. If you're at all familiar with the area around Second Street and Chandler, you know it's overrun with drug dealers, prostitutes, street people, gangs—you name it. It's so rough the police have almost given up patrolling it.

"But right in the middle of all that is a big, vacant four-story building, the old Jeffers Building. Paige, Inc., bought it several months ago along with some other commercial properties downtown. Rachel and I would like to see it turned into a sort of street ministry where people could hear preaching, but also find food, clothing, temporary shelter and maybe even medical help. We're thinking of calling it 'Southside Mission.'"

In the audience, Dr. West quickly nodded, her face alight. Jenny smiled at her.

"I have to admit that at first, this whole idea sounded more like a nightmare than a dream to me. I'm a businesswoman, not a missionary, and in the past I've done my best to avoid involving myself with these kinds of people. But lately, I've become convinced that I need to start giving *myself* rather than just my money."

She stopped, groping for the right words. "Most of you know that I have been blessed financially. I've always prided myself on giving generously to the church, sure that I was doing my Christian duty. Ever since I took this pledge, though,

I've started wondering. Is it really following Jesus to give away money you'll never miss? Or to support charities financially while refusing to get personally involved with the people they help? Where is the self-denial, the suffering, in that?"

She smiled gently. "So, here I am. I firmly believe the Lord has directed me to become involved with Southside Mission, and oddly enough, I'm starting to enjoy it! We hope to equip it with enough cots to sleep 125 and to have a dining area big enough to feed the same number. Pastor Maxwell has already talked to several other ministers in the area who might be willing to help. If all goes well, it should be ready to open within six weeks."

When Jenny sat down, a low murmur of excitement ran through the group. Dr. West leaned over to speak to Ted and Kim Newton; Lauren Woods and Terri Bannister also talked hurriedly. The idea of a street mission caught their imaginations. Suddenly, the very air suddenly seemed charged with divine possibilities.

Michael Maxwell stood up and motioned for silence. "Once the mission opens," he said, "there'll undoubtedly be a great need for counselors and workers. Please pray about it, and let me know if you'd like to have a part in that ministry."

A few minutes later, Michael asked Cliff Bright to close the meeting. As Cliff rose and began to pray in his soft, earnest fashion, a hush once again fell upon the room. A distinct wave of spiritual power moved over those gathered there, causing many of them to feel a sudden deep yearning, a hunger to walk the way of sacrifice, to suffer something for Jesus.

Who could resist such a baptism of power? How had they lived all these years without it?

13

RACHEL DROVE BACK TO HER APARTMENT LOST IN thought. The First Church after-meeting had left her curiously restless, unable to settle down to her Sunday afternoon routine of housecleaning and laundry. Instead, she decided to write a long overdue letter to her parents.

Sitting at her small oak desk, she opened the drawer and pulled out a pad of rose-colored stationery decorated with music notes. After thinking a moment, she started writing in her precise longhand:

Dear Mom and Dad,

Sorry it's taken me so long to write back to you, but a lot of exciting things have been going on here.

Last time we talked you were concerned about the church pledge I took, especially about whether I was getting into some kind of "cult" or "mind control" situation. I want you to know that nothing could be farther from the truth. In fact, if anything, this pledge has made me much more resistant to being pressured into things against my better judgment.

I'll give you one example, now that it's all over and I'm not still struggling with it.

Six weeks ago, a Chicago production company offered me a chance to audition for a part in a TV movie called *Secret Rage* to be filmed this summer. They had heard me sing in church and thought I'd be perfect for the part of a nightclub singer.

At first it sounded wonderful. The money was fantastic, and it would be a perfect opportunity to launch my singing career. The only problem was, both the movie and my part were, to say the least, morally questionable. On top of the unhealthy theme of the movie in general (a young man with multiple personalities kills both his parents), I'd have to swear and appear in at least one explicit "love" scene.

Still, I was going to do it anyway—until I remembered my pledge. To tell the truth, it made me mad at first to think that God would spoil something that exciting, and I came very close to breaking my promise so I could do what I wanted. I still don't know exactly what stopped me—unless it was the Holy Spirit.

I know, I know. That probably sounds very strange, especially coming from me! I've never been one to use "churchy" phrases like "Holy Ghost." In fact, if I ever thought about the Spirit at all, it was only in the vaguest terms, like some kind of religious theory.

But if there's any one thing I've learned over these last few months, Mom and Dad, it's that the Holy Spirit is real, the actual presence of God in my life. I mean—I feel now like I've spent years going through the motions of being a Christian without understanding where it all springs from, kind of like a flashlight trying to shine without batteries!

It's made a big difference in the way I pray. In the past, if I prayed at all, I never really expected to get an answer; it was more like positive thinking, "wishing" for things I wanted. But I can't tell you how many specific prayers I've seen answered just in these last few months alone, both for myself and for others. It's incredible!

Remember President Marshall out at my college? He took the pledge at First Church along with the rest of us, and several weeks ago he asked all of us to pray for a student who was having financial difficulties that might force him to drop out in his final semester. The poor guy was already working two jobs, but there was some kind of problem with his family. Anyway, we prayed that God would provide a way for him to stay in school and sure enough, he did! Lincoln College got a number of donations toward the student's tuition, and they added up to within twenty-five dollars of what he needed! Mr. Marshall made up the rest.

Then there's Ted Newton, the station manager at WFBB-TV. After he took the First Church pledge, he started running the station like he thought Jesus would—getting rid of some of the really offensive programs and trying to replace them with some wholesome family shows.

He came close to having to quit his job last month after he announced that he'd no longer accept heavily sex-oriented advertising. But despite our local newspaper's cynical comments about Ted's "Pollyanna ideas" and the other stations' victory parties, Channel 5's ratings immediately went up! Nobody in the business understands it, but that's a direct answer to our prayers.

And do you remember my mentioning Jenny Paige? She's a real estate developer whose family owns a lot of property in Ashton. She and I are working together now on a plan for a downtown outreach aimed at reaching Ashton's street people. Next time we talk I'll tell you all about it. We've got some really exciting ideas.

Anyway, I just wanted to let you know that everything is going well. I'll try harder from now on to stay in touch so you won't worry. Give all my love to Gram and Gramps, and tell Jimmy to stay out of trouble.

Much love,
Rachel

After a moment's hesitation, she added:

P.S. Jason also sends his love, and says he's looking forward to seeing you when we visit in November.

At that same moment, Jason Clark was also contemplating his and Rachel's plans to spend the Thanksgiving holiday with her family.

Sitting at the piano in his apartment, his long fingers skillfully stroked the keys to create a soft, sensual melody that closely echoed his thoughts. He paused briefly to make a note on the half-filled music sheet propped in front of him, smiling at the scrawled song title: "Rachel."

The lyrics he'd composed were as throbbingly suggestive as the music he played:

Sweet perfume fills the air
Sunlight glints on auburn hair.
A promise in your lovely eyes
of us together—Paradise!

I'm a moth drawn to your fire
Beauty fills me with desire
No voice but yours can blend with mine
Our voices . . . bodies . . . all entwined.

That morning, he had decided at the last minute not to tell Pastor Maxwell exactly why he was leaving so hurriedly after the service. With Rachel's birthday just weeks away, he needed time to finish the song he planned to present her as a gift. Although he considered it a perfectly valid reason for missing the after-meeting, Jason somehow doubted Pastor Maxwell would agree.

Maybe I should go ahead and give her the engagement ring we picked out, too, he thought. *She's been acting a little strange toward me lately; that might smooth things out.*

Her parents would probably expect them to delay any announcement of an engagement until after the Thanksgiving visit to officially ask their "blessing," but he suddenly didn't want to delay any longer. *They'll get over it,* he decided, and with that confident thought returned to his music.

14

It was Friday night, and the crowd at the colorful Mardi Gras Pub was boisterous. Roger Paige walked through the door to be greeted enthusiastically by the other regular patrons.

As he made his way through the noisy, smoke-filled room, Jo Lynn, the tall barmaid, called cheerfully, "Hi, honey. How ya doin'?"

"Great," Roger replied, shouting to be heard over the country music band. "How about you?"

"'Bout the same. Life goes on."

Roger smiled an acknowledgment, then made his way over to a table where two of his racquetball buddies were already sipping drinks. Jo Lynn sat a drink in front of him, then flashed him a bright smile before disappearing back through the crowd.

After nodding companionably at Bruce and Dennis, Roger quickly scanned the packed room, spotting many familiar faces. The Mardi Gras drew a predictable crowd each weekend, mostly the younger, "work hard, play hard" set. The description fit Roger perfectly.

Tonight, though, he found himself once again battling restlessness. The conversations around him were all the same—forced, almost desperate gaiety that thinly concealed dark undertones of hopelessness. What was it with him lately? It was like nothing satisfied him any more. Even the music was depressing.

Maybe it's time for a vacation, he thought gloomily. *I haven't been diving for a while. I could take a week off and fly down to Cozumel—*

His thoughts stopped there abruptly. The last time he'd gone diving, it had been with Lisa. She'd made it plain at that time that marriage was on her mind. He'd made it equally plain that he wasn't interested in commitment. He'd heard since then that she'd become engaged to a stockbroker.

Better him than me, Roger thought bitingly. *I'm not ready to be tied down to just one woman yet.*

As if to contradict that thought, however, an image instantly sprang to his mind of wide, green eyes and auburn hair: Rachel.

Sipping his drink moodily, Roger recalled the way her eyes had sparkled as she talked about the church and the plans for Southside Mission. Rachel Wingate, he realized, had never acted particularly impressed with him, or like she even cared to be around him. He wasn't used to being so easily dismissed.

I'd like to get to know her better, he suddenly realized, somewhat to his surprise. *But I guess she and Jason Clark are pretty much committed. I don't know what it is about her, but she's really something.*

Over the next few weeks, First Church experienced an almost unprecedented flurry of activity. Volunteers made repeated excursions to the south side to work on the mission:

painting it inside and out, tearing out and replacing worn kitchen fixtures, laying new carpet, and bringing in chairs, tables, and cots donated by sister churches.

Daniel Marshall astonished everyone with his untiring dedication to the project.

"It's not what you might think," he admitted to Michael Maxwell. "I'm not even sure this whole concept of a street mission can be made to work. But I've taught theology for years and written books about 'practical Christianity' and 'imitating Christ' without even considering that *I* could be more actively involved. I've always assumed that I was supposed to serve the Lord in Christian education, where I'm best qualified. But lately I've felt that I should be getting more involved in the secular community. This looks like a good way to do that."

Maxwell nodded. "I'm glad you're helping out," he said. "I've already heard two or three people comment that you've provided a cool head and logical approach to the work that needs to be done. And I guess you're responsible for all the Lincoln students who are showing up to help—a lot of them don't even come to First Church."

The college president nodded. "I've talked out at the college about what we're doing and invited some of them to help. I'm glad they're getting involved." The concerted efforts to prepare the mission to open were covered one night on Channel 5's evening news.

"An unusual sight is being observed in Ashton's south side these days," the young reporter announced. "A dilapidated building on the corner of Chandler and Second is being transformed, almost overnight, into a 'street ministry' called Southside Mission, due to open next week. The winos and street gangs who roam the area seem bewildered by the flood of middle-class churchgoers and Lincoln Christian College students who boldly park their cars next to burned-out buildings and greet them with smiles and comments like 'Jesus loves you.'

"I'm here with Jenny Paige, whose company, Paige, Inc., donated the facility."

The camera scanned the newly painted Jeffers Building, an oasis among the other dirty, graffiti-scrawled buildings on the street. The lens brutally captured the sight of the homeless, some severely emaciated, sprawled sleeping on "beds" of rags on the sidewalks. Then the camera turned to Jenny.

"The mission will serve dinner each evening to up to 125 people immediately after the church service," she said, "and issue clothing and shoes to those who need them. Up to one hundred people will be able to check in for the night, shower, wash and dry their clothes, and sleep on a clean cot. Dr. Patricia West has also agreed to donate one afternoon a week to provide *pro bono* medical services."

"How is the mission being funded?"

"We debated about taking money from some charity organizations, but decided against it because of all the strings attached. At this time, the mission is funded entirely by private donations. We've already received food, money, and clothing from over fifteen churches in the area as well as from various individuals and even one Girl Scout troop. No tax money is involved."

"Are there any rules about who gets to stay overnight?"

"Well, they have to be sober," Jenny replied wryly. "And to get a bed they'll have to attend the evening church service and be willing to abide by the 'house rules'—including leaving their weapons at the door."

"Do you think they'll do that?"

"I think they will. Besides, we'll return their things when they leave. Our goal goes beyond just feeding or clothing or disarming them; we want to see their lives changed. Once that happens, the rest will follow."

The news clip ended with some brief footage of Lincoln College students washing some newly replaced windows while black-clad gang members nearby made obscene gestures at the camera. It was a vivid image of stark contrasts, both promising and unsettling.

It was Wednesday evening, two days before the scheduled opening of Southside Mission, and the mid-week service at First Church of Ashton was unusually crowded. As Michael greeted people at the door, he marveled at how many new faces he saw. Many appeared to be young people, some recognizable as Lincoln students.

Connie Garza came up the steps, her face alight as she introduced Michael to her husband. Epimenio Garza, gaunt but smiling, shook the pastor's hand.

"Connie's been trying to get me to church for months now," he said. "Her boss comes here, and she's really been enjoying it. I figured it was about time I came along."

Michael grinned. "Glad to have you. I almost feel like I already know you—we've been praying for your recovery at the Sunday after-meetings."

Epimenio nodded, embarrassed. "Connie told me. I don't know that much about church, but she says you people have really helped her. All this has been pretty hard for us."

Michael shook the man's hand again. *We're starting to function as the body of Christ,* he thought excitedly. *This is what the church is supposed to be all about.*

That Friday night, Southside Mission officially opened its doors. Fliers had been posted throughout the area announcing the first service, and by late afternoon the mouth-watering aromas of freshly baked bread and simmering beef stew filled the city streets. As the six o'clock opening hour approached, a varied crowd began to gather on the sidewalk outside. The southsiders, ranging from obviously drunken elderly men to arrogant teenagers to wary, hard-faced women, jostled for position and eyed each other with varying degrees of hostility. It was a potentially explosive mix.

At exactly six, Jenny Paige and Michael Maxwell unlocked the front doors. There was an instant stampede, but it slowed a moment later when the first ones in reached the "check-in" station. Lauren Woods and two other First Church volunteers stood behind a counter, pleasantly explaining that mission rules required that all weapons, alcohol, and "controlled substances" be stowed in lockers before going inside.

The first man glared at Lauren. "You gonna take my bottle while I eat!" he said accusingly. When Lauren assured him that he could take the locker key with him he still hesitated, but finally the smell of lasagna and freshly baked bread from inside won him over. He grudgingly shoved his small bottle in a locker and went into the dining hall.

It was set up cafeteria style, with plastic trays and a serving line. Michael Maxwell watched unobtrusively from the far side of the room as the street people, the vast majority of them men, shoved their way through the line. The younger ones were treating it like a joke, laughing and sneering at the "church freaks" who were stupid enough to give away food.

"It prob'ly make them feel real good to help us po' hungry niggers," one remarked. "We be doin' 'em a big favor, eatin' this ______." The expletive he used to describe the free meal drew sharp glances from the volunteers in the serving line.

"Yeah," another smirked. "And have you looked at these church women? I think they need a man." He leaned forward to leer suggestively at an older volunteer in the serving line. As he graphically described what he'd like to do, her eyes grew wide. The man burst out laughing and moved on.

Michael felt sudden doubt. Was it wise to expose the volunteers to such men and their crude language? The mission was such a small light in the midst of such great darkness; was it really worth the risk?

And yet, he knew the Holy Spirit had the power to melt even the hardest hearts, replace lust and hatred with perfect love. *This is where we belong,* he thought firmly, *with the same sick and sinful people Jesus reached out to.*

At seven o'clock, the evening service began in the chapel adjoining the dining hall. Those still eating looked up in surprise when they heard catchy music starting, and most went into the chapel, where about thirty-five people were already assembled. Jenny Paige was seated on the front row with Dr. West, Daniel Marshall, and a half-dozen other First Church members who'd come for the mission's first service. The room quickly filled as the latecomers noisily pressed inside.

When Rachel Wingate stepped up onto the small elevated stage, she was instantly met with a chorus of loud wolf whistles and drunken shouts. Ignoring them, she picked up a microphone as the pianist played the opening chords to "All to Thee."

The whistling and shouts abruptly died away as soon as Rachel started singing.

I have heard the voice of Jesus
calling clearly "Follow Me";
No one else could ever promise
*Life eternal and so free.**

The hardened crowd seemed riveted by the purity and sweetness of her voice. One wizened old man started sniffling, rubbing his bleary eyes with the back of his hand as he listened. Several young men wearing black bandannas knotted on their heads stared at the floor, scowling in an obvious effort to deny any emotional response.

Tho' unworthy of salvation,
Jesus sought me for His own;
On the cross He died to save me,
Now I long to make Him known.

Only Jesus is the answer
For the happiness we seek;
He alone can lift life's burden,
And give strength unto the weak.

Rachel was surprised when Jason Clark walked in and glanced around; she somehow hadn't expected him to show up. Her heart suddenly light, she asked the crowd to stand and join her in singing the chorus:

All to Thee, I give my all to Thee,
All to Thee, Thine only will I be;
All to Thee, O Christ of Calvary,
My prayer shall ever be, my all to Thee.

When the music faded, she handed the microphone to Pastor Maxwell. As she quietly stepped down from the stage to go sit beside Jason, she was startled by a deep voice that boomed: "Praise the Lord!" Heads turned toward the speaker, a tall, heavyset black man at the back of the room wearing a tattered shirt and cap. He smiled beatifically, revealing several gaps where his front teeth should have been. A ripple of laughter ran through the audience.

The moment Michael tried to speak, however, the ugly mood returned to the crowd. A harsh, almost angry murmur started across the room—whispers of "rev'rend from First Church" . . . , "big, fancy place in north Ashton . . . ," "rich white church"— and soon grew into drunken shouts.

"We don't need no fancy preacher in the south side!" someone shouted, while another called out, "Why don't you people stay in north Ashton where you belong?" A large man with a beard provoked gales of laughter by standing up to sing "Amazing Grace" in loud, nasal tones, gesturing for emphasis. "Hey, preacher," a woman shouted, "we got us a deal with God, see—we leave Him alone, and He leave us alone!"

Michael tried to regain control by raising his hands, then his voice, but it was hopeless. They were arguing and milling around, not even listening. In one corner two men started angrily shoving each other.

Finally, Michael stepped down from the stage and walked over to the small First Church group. Sitting on a folding chair, he covered his face with his hands and began to pray.

Rachel touched his shoulder. "Pastor Maxwell, should I sing again? Maybe that would calm them down."

Michael, near despair, looked up. "Thanks, Rachel. Maybe they'll listen to you."

She leaped up and quickly mounted the steps to the stage again, followed closely by the pianist. A moment later her clear voice was once again raised in song:

When peace, like a river, attendeth my way,
When sorrows like sea billows roll;
Whatever my lot, Thou hast taught me to say,
It is well, it is well with my soul.

She hadn't sung the first line before the southsiders were all turned toward her, sadly thoughtful, listening almost against their will. Before she finished the verse, the room was subdued and tamed. It lay like some wild beast at her feet as she sang it into harmlessness, her lovely face radiant.

Michael watched the transformation of the mob with awe, catching a sudden glimpse of what Jesus could do with a voice like Rachel's. It was a gift that could touch and heal those around her, that could bring peace in the midst of strife.

Dear Lord, he prayed, *lead her faithfully in the path You'd have her take. Let her life reflect Your great love.*

A few seats away, Jason Clark's eyes were also fixed on the singer. Unlike Michael, he was thinking that Rachel had never looked more beautiful, more appealing. His thoughts drifted into anticipation, and he smiled confidently as he recalled the words he'd written: "*our voices . . . bodies . . . entwined.*"

No one noticed the unlikely presence of Roger Paige, who stood unobtrusively just inside the chapel door. On impulse, he'd left the Mardi Gras early to visit the mission opening that Rachel and his mother had talked so much about. Now, as he watched the young singer step down and Michael Maxwell turn to face the subdued crowd, he saw again the indefinable strength, the joyful radiance, in both their faces.

He hesitated for a moment, then turned to leave as quietly as he'd arrived. Neither Rachel nor his mother saw him as he slipped back outside and drove away.

Michael stood in front of the crowded room, feeling calmer this time. What would Jesus do before this kind of audience? Christianity had to be more than delivering slick, "professional" sermons to smug audiences who were already converted. Wasn't it about calling lost and weary sinners like these to repentance? How would He speak to these people?

Michael didn't realize it, but the deep compassion he felt showed plainly on his face, commanding the attention of his restless audience. Empowered by the Spirit, he spoke as never before of the love Jesus had for them and what a rich life He promised for those who became His followers.

When the meeting closed two hours later, the chapel quickly emptied, most of the southsiders heading back to the streets that spawned them. Only a handful stayed behind, among them Eddie Saenz, a painfully thin Puerto Rican teenager wearing a black bandanna on his head.

He approached Michael hesitantly. "I sleep here tonight?" he asked in broken English. "No cost me nothin'?" His voice, like his movements, was disjointed, and he jumped when two older teenagers also wearing bandannas moved close to him and spoke sharply in Spanish. It was evident that they were pressuring him to leave with them.

"You can stay for free," Michael confirmed. "You have to shower before getting a bed, and be up and out by seven o'clock tomorrow morning. If you stay, you'll get breakfast in the morning before you go. You can wash and dry your clothes here if you want, but if you leave tonight, you can't get back in. The doors are locked at nine o'clock."

Eddie listened carefully, then shot a nervous glance at his companions before bobbing his head twice, quickly. "Okay," he said. "Okay, I stay." After another sharp exchange in Spanish, his friends stormed out.

Eddie's hands visibly trembled as he turned back to Michael and searched for words. "I—I don' wan' be with them no more," he said with an effort. Dr. West had remained after the service, and she'd witnessed the entire exchange. Now she said quietly, "Look at his arm. That's why he's got the shakes so bad." Needle marks covered the teenager's forearms. She stepped closer to Eddie. "How old are you, son?"

The boy looked at her, then dropped his eyes. "*Quince*," he murmured. Dr. West glanced at Michael, horrified. On the streets and an addict at only fifteen years old!

She turned to Michael decisively. "He'll need medical help and close monitoring, but I'm not scheduled for the clinic here until late next week. Do you think someone could bring him into my office first thing in the morning?"

"I'm sure we can arrange that, as long as he'll cooperate. Thanks a lot, Pat, for being here tonight."

"Wouldn't have missed it for the world," she said cheerfully. "See you later."

When Michael finally left at almost ten o'clock that night, there were less than a dozen men signed into the men's dormitory—equipped for more than seventy—and no women at all. Not one person had responded to the altar call at the end of the service.

Driving away through the dark streets, Michael mused about the events of that night, his disappointment tempered by the memory of Eddie's amazement that the "lady doctor" would treat him for free, and a frail elderly man's gratitude at being given a clean blanket. Winter was approaching, and soon the street people would be huddling over trash fires to stay warm. Southside Mission could literally be a lifeline for those most vulnerable—the very old and very young.

He was turning a corner when he spotted a heavily made-up teenage girl he recognized from the service, laughing and talking to a balding man in a red Porsche. As he watched, she walked around and got into the car, smoothing her tight skirt with skill. The two quickly disappeared into the night.

With a sinking heart Michael realized that he'd just witnessed a prostitute being solicited. *Dear God,* he cried silently, *this place is like a festering sore. Show me how to reach these people with Your love!*

After the service ended that evening, Jason Clark had asked Rachel if he could take her home. Since she'd driven in early that afternoon with Jenny, her own car was at home. She gratefully accepted.

She was unusually quiet as they drove through the dark city streets. Jason reached over and gently pulled her toward him.

"Come over here," he said. "I haven't seen much of you lately because of all this mission stuff. Don't you miss me?"

Rachel unbuckled her seat belt and scooted over next to him, resting her head against his shoulder with a contented sigh. "Yes, I sure do. I was really happy you came tonight, Jason. I didn't expect you to show up."

He laughed. "Well, it wasn't exactly my idea of an exciting place to spend a Friday night, but since *you* were there . . ."

He let his words trail off as he leaned down to quickly brush her cheek with his lips. "When I walked in and saw you singing in front of all those filthy people, it was like stumbling across a diamond in—in a garbage heap! I wanted to sweep you out of that ugly place and—"

He impulsively rolled to a stop in the middle of the quiet street and drew her close to him, but even as his lips hungrily sought hers, he felt her stiffen in his arms. Irritated, he drew back and looked at her.

"What's the matter with you?" he demanded angrily. "I thought you said you missed me!"

She looked miserable. "I do, Jason," she said. "I guess I'm just not in the mood right now."

He put the car back in gear with a jerk and started forward again, speeding down the dark streets. Rachel studied his angry profile thoughtfully.

"Didn't you see those people in there tonight?" she finally asked. "Didn't you *feel* anything about them other than their 'filthiness'? A lot of them live in the streets, Jason, literally sleeping on the sidewalks. Some of them are borderline mentally ill and can't even care for themselves. They need help, and hope—and most of all, they need to know Jesus."

Jason gave her a sideways glance, and she suddenly felt embarrassed. To him, her impassioned words must have sounded incredibly naive.

"You're really into all this, aren't you?" he asked. "You've been acting different lately. I'm not sure I even know you anymore."

She looked back at him, unable to think of a response. *You seem different, too,* she thought. *Or maybe I'm just seeing you in a different light.*

They rode the rest of the way home in uncomfortable silence. When they finally pulled up at Rachel's apartment, Jason got out and walked her to the door.

"Listen," he said abruptly, placing his hands on her shoulders, "I'm sorry, okay? Lately everything I say to you seems to be wrong. I didn't mean to get you upset." His face was suddenly soft, his voice persuasive. "Can we just forget all this and go on? I'd planned a big surprise for your birthday tomorrow, and I don't want it to be spoiled by some silly misunderstanding. You know I'd never deliberately do anything to hurt or upset you."

He lifted her chin, forcing her to look him in the eyes. "Forgive me?" he asked ruefully.

His boyish grin and repentant manner made Rachel smile despite herself. "Okay, okay," she said, standing on tiptoe to give him a quick placatory kiss on the cheek. "And I *am* glad you came tonight. What time are you picking me up tomorrow?"

"I'll be here at five." He gathered her close for a gentle, lingering hug, then slowly released her, giving her a tender look that left her flushed.

"See you then," he said softly.

Rachel waved as he drove off, then went inside and bolted the door. But as she moved through the apartment absently straightening magazines and carrying a dirty cup into the kitchen, the vague uneasiness she'd felt in the car slowly returned. What was it about Jason that left her so unsettled? She loved him, wanted to spend the rest of her life with him—didn't she?

Pulling a clean mug from the cabinet, she went to the kitchen sink and turned the water on, letting it run over her fingers as she waited for it to warm up. She hoped relaxing with some hot tea would help her see things more clearly.

Lost in thought, she didn't notice how quickly the water was heating up. By the time she shouted, "Ouch!" and belatedly jerked her hand back, her slender fingers were scalded. Tears abruptly welled in her eyes—but not just because of her fingers. Wrapping a dish towel around her hand, she walked into her room and sat on the edge of the bed.

Oh, Jason, she silently cried, *I love you so much. Why do you leave me so confused?*

15

THE SUNDAY AFTER-MEETING WAS MORE CROWDED than ever, despite the overcast weather. Fall was setting in, and the bright greens of summer were slowly changing to autumn hues. The air was slightly damp.

Inside the First Church sanctuary, people were still milling around exchanging greetings. Alex and Cheryl Powell were chatting with an older couple attending for the first time; Lauren Woods and Terri Bannister huddled near the front talking animatedly. Terri's husband, Ray, had come to church with her and the kids that morning for the first time, so she'd be leaving early. Jason stood with a possessive arm around Rachel as she and Kim Newton discussed some of Ted's latest ideas for Channel 5. Cliff Bright and Jenny Paige, their faces grim, appeared to be engaged in a serious conversation.

When Michael called the meeting to order, they all quickly found seats. Daniel Marshall opened with prayer, then Michael began to tell about the first service at Southside Mission.

"I think that most of us who went there Friday night saw and heard things that made us uncomfortable," he said, "but I think we also became a lot more aware of the kind of problems that exist in the south side. Many of the young people in the area are dropouts who've either run away or been thrown out of abusive homes, and they've gone to the only people who take an interest in them—the pimps and pushers. Others have ended up in street gangs.

"I talked at length with a fifteen-year-old boy named Eddie who joined a gang called the 'Second Streets' over a year ago. Several of them came to the mission Friday night to eat and cause trouble, but Eddie ended up staying for the night. He went to see Dr. West yesterday to begin drug treatment."

Michael smiled at Patricia West. "Eddie doesn't speak much English, but Dr. West tells me he's been asking a lot of questions about '*el Cristo*.' We need to find someone who speaks Spanish to talk with him in more detail."

Several rows back, Connie and Epimenio Garza exchanged a quick glance. Connie raised her hand.

"Pastor Maxwell? 'Menio and I could talk to him—," then she added, casting an impish smile in Cliff Bright's direction, "if I can convince my boss to let me off early some afternoon."

Cliff's troubled face momentarily cleared. "I think that can be arranged," he said, grinning back at her.

"Great!" said Michael. "Jenny, can you help them get together with Eddie?" Jenny Paige nodded.

Terri Bannister raised her hand. "How many of the southsiders responded to the altar call on Friday?"

"No one came forward either Friday or Saturday," Michael admitted, "but I don't think we should be discouraged by that. The south side has been a stronghold of evil for a long time, and it'll probably take awhile to break through that. But

I talked to Pastor Snyder from Ashton Park Baptist early this morning—he preached at the mission yesterday—and he said that two of the men who stayed last night prayed later to receive Jesus."

There was an excited spatter of applause. Michael waited for it to die down.

"We need to remember the mission in prayer," he said. "I've committed to preaching the Friday night services for the next three months, but Jenny tells me they need volunteers during the week to help with some of the kitchen and maintenance duties as well as with counseling. Right now they've only got three permanent staff members."

He paused then and glanced around until he located Rachel and Jason. "Now," he said, "I think there are two people here who'd like to share some exciting news. Jason? Rachel?"

With self-conscious smiles, the young couple rose and turned to face the crowd. Jason smiled down at Rachel, then gently took her left hand in his.

"Last night, I took Rachel out to a nice restaurant to celebrate her birthday," he said, "and after the meal I had roses brought to our table. While she still had her arms full of flowers, I got down on my knees in front of everyone and asked her to marry me."

A murmur of satisfied approval ran through the crowd, and several people laughed. Jason proudly lifted Rachel's hand high to display the sparkling diamond ring on her finger.

"She probably just said yes to keep from embarrassing me," he said modestly, "but now she's stuck with me. Since we've talked about getting married for almost a year now, we've decided not to put it off too long. We're tentatively planning a December wedding, and we'd like all of you to come."

This time the applause turned into cheers and congratulatory shouts. Only Jenny Paige, studying Rachel closely, caught the fleeting expression—was it doubt?—that shadowed her lovely face. The next instant, however, as Rachel smiled up at Jason, she looked as radiantly happy as any newly-engaged young woman.

After they sat down, Ted Newton stood up to share his news about a new local series WFBB-TV would soon launch called "The Hero Next Door."

"It'll be similar to some of the other 'reality shows' that are so popular right now, but with a different twist," he said. "Instead of featuring trained rescuers doing their jobs, it'll focus on ordinary people who, in a moment of crisis, willingly risk their lives for strangers—like the Chicago man last year who helped a woman being attacked by armed muggers, or the two high school students who jumped into a fast-moving river to rescue a toddler trapped inside a sinking car. Ordinary people doing extraordinary things—or, in Christian terms, 'doing unto others as you'd have them do unto you.' It won't be overtly religious, but many of these 'heroes' appear to have a strong element of Christian faith in their lives. At the very least, it'll be an encouraging, uplifting show, some good news in a bad news world."

After Ted sat down, Michael commented, "Well, it sounds like God is really moving in people's lives! Anybody else have anything to share today before we close? A prayer request or another testimony?"

Jenny looked pointedly at Cliff Bright. The store owner sighed and slowly stood up.

"I hate even to share this after all the exciting news," he said, "but I guess I need to. Remember last month when I mentioned that, due to the financial losses my company had suffered because of changes I'd made, I might have to close several stores? I know many of you have made it a point to shop at Mr. B Stores since then, and I really appreciate your efforts, but unfortunately it's still not been enough. Next week my Ray Street and Sunset stores will close."

The announcement was met with a moment of stunned silence. Several people turned to look at Connie Garza, knowing she worked at Mr. B. She shook her head; neither of the stores being closed was hers.

Cliff went on, "I'm hoping that, by downsizing now, I can prevent any more store closings from becoming necessary. But I have to tell you—" His voice broke, and he had to clear his throat and wait a moment before continuing. "I have to tell you that this has been very difficult. Elizabeth doesn't understand why I'm doing this, and she—she—"

This time it took him longer to regain control of his speech. As he stood, his balding head half bowed, Michael walked over to put a hand on his shoulder; Alex Powell and Daniel Marshall quickly followed suit. When the store owner looked up again, he was surrounded with supporters.

"Cliff," Michael said, "I don't know what to say. I wish I had some kind of answers for you to make it all easier, but I don't. Can we just pray for you, and for Elizabeth?"

Cliff nodded wordlessly. Michael, his hand still firmly on Cliff's shoulder, closed his eyes and bowed his head.

"Lord, we know that You're present in our midst, and that You're intimately aware of all the setbacks Cliff has encountered as he's tried to honor his pledge to follow You. We don't understand why his faithfulness in business seems to have been rewarded with failure, or why his devotion to You has brought such pain and strife to his home. But regardless of how it looks, we know that You're a good and loving Father who works all things together for good. Lord Jesus, please let this whole situation somehow work for Cliff's and Elizabeth's good."

There was a moment of silence, then Alex Powell's deep voice quietly continued the prayer, "Dear Lord, we want to stand with our brother in this difficult time. Please grant him Your strength and peace in the days and weeks to come, and show the rest of us what we can do to help bear his burden."

One by one, various others spoke out to ask God's peace and blessing on Cliff, and to intercede on his behalf. There was an almost tangible sense of the Spirit's presence in the room, and by the time the prayer ended there were few dry eyes. When people slowly looked up, still half distracted, the unseen bond between them brought to mind the words of Psalm 133:1: "Behold, how good and how pleasant it is for brethren to dwell together in unity" (KJV).

September turned to October, leaves fell, and the weather turned cold. In the south side, the poor and homeless braced for another long winter of hardship.

But this year, the word was slowly circulating in the streets: Southside Mission was "for real," a safe place to find food, clothing, and medical help. In the three weeks since it had opened, the mission had gone from housing less than a dozen men to more than fifty each night, and seventeen men and two women had made the decision to follow Christ. The women's section still remained largely vacant, though, and fully a third of the new converts had soon disappeared back into the streets. To everyone's sorrow, young Eddie Saenz was one of them.

On this Friday night, the dining hall was crowded to capacity with people driven inside by the season's first snowfall. Michael Maxwell noticed many new faces, but he had learned enough by now not to approach them directly. Southsiders were, of necessity, wary.

The minister had also learned not to show up in a suit and tie. Tonight he wore jeans, tennis shoes, and a pullover sweater. At first it had felt odd and uncomfortable to preach in such casual garb, but he had finally adopted the apostle Paul's attitude: "I have become all things to all men, so that by all possible means I might save some."

Now, moving through the crowd, he warmly greeted some of the "regulars." "Hi, Nick," he called to a tiny, birdlike elderly man huddled in a corner with a plate of lasagna.

Nick looked up, his gray face lighting up in a smile. "Hi, Father," he answered. "Nice dinner tonight." Michael grinned and shook his head; the man, who was mildly retarded, had been raised Catholic, and no amount of explanation could shake his habit of referring to him as "Father Maxwell."

More women were present than usual, both the older "bag lady" variety and some of the district's many prostitutes. *It must be the cold that's driving them inside,* Michael thought. *Maybe we should pray for a long winter!*

At 7:30 the evening service began. This time when Rachel nimbly stepped up on the stage and motioned to the pianist, there were only a few ribald shouts and wolf whistles. Those seated around the troublemakers quickly quieted them as Rachel picked up the microphone. Over the past few weeks that she'd been coming to sing, the southsiders had grown increasingly respectful toward Rachel, impressed by the unselfish giving of her time and talent.

She started the service tonight with a fast-moving song called "Suddenly Eternity."

We all go through this life
as if we're here to stay,
Making plans, working hard,
taking it day by day.

We all think that someday soon
we'll take time to make things right,
But when that call comes through for you
it's like a thief in the night!

Suddenly eternity! Your plans have gone astray.
Suddenly eternity! Today is the day.
Suddenly eternity! What you are is all you will be.
There is no more time . . . There is suddenly eternity.

The southsiders listened with varying degrees of visible response. A thirtyish woman wearing a tight, black jacket looked stricken, as if she'd just caught a horrifying glimpse into her future; a man a few years older stared, unseeing, at his own hands. Rachel started into the second verse:

But if we try to live our lives
as if each day is the last,
If we put our trust in Him,
hold our commitments fast.

Someday when that moment comes
that our lives will be required . . .
We won't have to be ashamed
in that sudden hour!

By the time she'd finished the second chorus, she had the undivided attention of every person in the room. When Michael stood up to speak, he sensed immediately that something was different tonight; the normally rowdy audience was as quiet as his affluent and sophisticated First Church congregation ever was.

That Friday night there occurred some of the most remarkable scenes he and his small group from First Church had ever witnessed. Although there was nothing especially new in his simple message of God's love and forgiveness, as the Holy Spirit swept across the room, the hardened audience was unaccountably touched. Before he was finished speaking, there were the sounds of open weeping in the crowd. When Rachel finally rose and began to sing, the southsiders moved almost as one toward the platform.

Softly and tenderly, Jesus is calling,
Calling for you and for me . . .
See, on the portals He's waiting and watching,
Watching for you and for me

Come home, come home!
Ye who are weary, come home
Earnestly, tenderly, Jesus is calling,
Calling, O sinner, come home!"

Michael hardly said a word. Stretching out his hand with a gesture of invitation, he waited for all those who stumbled forward, weeping, to kneel at the front. As he went among them to pray, he saw Jenny Paige kneeling with an older woman and Rachel Wingate holding a weeping young prostitute.

As the southsiders continued to crowd in a double row around the platform, a well-dressed young man suddenly pushed his way through to kneel among them. Michael, catching sight of him, stared in astonishment. It was Roger Paige.

It was nearly midnight before the service ended. Michael stayed up long into Saturday morning, praying and talking with many of the new converts who, bewildered by the emotional upheaval they'd just experienced, clung to him as though their lives depended upon his physical presence. Roger Paige was among those who stayed.

Rachel had spoken to Roger briefly before she and Jason left. Her face was soft as she approached and extended both her hands to him.

"I'm so happy for you," she said quietly, her eyes shining with tears. "Your mom and I have prayed for you so often."

Roger awkwardly took her hands in his own. "Thanks," he murmured. "I don't know why I ran from God for so long. Guess I was just being stubborn."

He glanced over to where his mother sat counseling a young woman. Feeling his gaze she glanced up, her weary face reflecting her joy at his presence. He smiled at her before turning back to Rachel.

"You and Mom—you were really the ones who got to me," he said. "That night at my house, when you were talking about the mission, all of a sudden it seemed so—*real.* You were both so happy! I couldn't figure it out." He laughed suddenly, his face alight with new joy. "Now I think I know what the excitement was all about."

Rachel grinned, then impulsively stepped forward to give him a hug. She was startled when Jason stepped forward to intercept her.

"Hey, what's this?" he said only half-jokingly, putting his arm possessively around her shoulders. "Go find your own girl, Paige. This one's mine."

His words embarrassed Rachel. "Jason, stop it. I was just congratulating him. He came to know the Lord tonight! Isn't that great?"

"Yeah, sure, that's great." After only a moment's hesitation he put out his hand, and Roger shook it warmly.

Jason abruptly turned back to Rachel. "We really need to go now. Are you ready?"

"I guess so. See you at church on Sunday, Roger?"

Roger nodded. "Yeah, see you then."

It wasn't until they were in the car that Jason asked tersely, "Why'd you do that?"

Rachel looked at him, puzzled. "Why'd I do what?"

"Grab Roger like that. You're supposed to be engaged to me. I wish you'd start acting like it!"

Rachel stared at him in utter astonishment. "What are you talking about? Didn't you even see what happened there tonight? Didn't you feel the presence of the Holy Spirit? It was the most powerful, most awesome—"

Words momentarily escaped her. How could he have sat in the same room, watched all those men's and women's lives be transformed and yet remain untouched?

Her thoughts turned to the sights they had witnessed earlier that night: the tear-stained face of the "fallen woman" Jenny had enfolded in her arms as she gently led her to the Savior and the shining face of the elderly man who had knelt beside Michael to exchange his life of drunken debauchery for a new life as a child of the King. And Roger Paige's humbled expression as he knelt among the people Jason had once referred to as "garbage." Those faces—men and women touched, for the first time, with the Spirit's glory!

Studying Jason's stony profile, Rachel realized with sudden, painful clarity that he had no respect at all for the supernatural events they had witnessed. She felt a sudden sense of revulsion. All the time she had been singing with the complete passion of her soul, he had been unmoved—except, perhaps, for his longing to physically possess her. She unconsciously twisted the diamond ring on her slender finger, suddenly feeling smothered. "Take me home," she said. "*Now.*"

16

Once inside her apartment, Rachel hardly remembered telling Jason goodnight. She paced restlessly, trying in vain to sort through her conflicting emotions.

Did she truly love him? Had she ever? *Yes. No.* "I don't know!" she finally whispered aloud, then stopped, appalled at her own words.

Sinking onto the couch, she hugged her knees, tears streaming down her cheeks. What was the matter with her? Jason was handsome, charming, the perfect companion. When she was with him, he made everything seem so right.

But that's part of the problem, she thought, remembering how he'd urged her to take the movie part even though it meant "temporarily" compromising her morals. It had seemed right when he'd explained it, and yet—it was just plain wrong!

With that thought, she walked over to the stereo and slid a hand-labeled cassette into the tape player. When the music started, she settled back on the couch and closed her eyes to listen.

Sweet perfume fills the air
Sunlight glints on auburn hair . . .

As Jason's smooth tenor voice sang the words that had so thrilled her when he sang them to her, she discovered she felt curiously detached. Why wasn't it moving her?

I'm a moth drawn to your fire
Beauty fills me with desire . . .

Suddenly nauseated, Rachel leaped up and jabbed the "stop" button—then stood frozen, lost in thought.

What was Jason really to her, or she to him? Undeniably, they both felt a strong physical attraction. But, beneath his easy charm and wit, was there the inner strength and determination of a man truly committed to the Lord? Most important of all, did she respect him enough to give him her trust, her life?

"No. No!" she said aloud, and with those words she knew her choice had been made.

The realization brought an instant cloud of distressing thoughts. She and Jason had made so many plans together—picked out their living room furniture, imagined the kind of house they'd buy, even chosen names for their "first few" kids. She couldn't even imagine a future that didn't include Jason. Without him, all her most cherished dreams were dead.

And what about all the people at church? They'd been so excited about their engagement! And her parents—they'd already sent the plane tickets for her and Jason's visit at Thanksgiving, less than a week away. How could she just cancel out like this at the last minute?

Despite all the dark and confusing thoughts, however, she suddenly felt a strange sense of relief. Deep in her heart she knew she'd made the right decision, regardless of the pain it brought. She'd just have to face the consequences as they came. She slipped the diamond ring from her finger and carefully placed it on the corner of her desk. She'd get a few hours of sleep, then go talk to Jason.

There was a heightened sense of excitement among First Church members that Sunday morning. News of the revival that struck Southside had swiftly spread, and the attendance, which had been tapering off for months, was slightly up.

Michael faced the congregation with a deep sense of humility and gratitude, aware that a new, unspoken camaraderie was developing between them. The more literal imitation of Jesus that had begun with a small group of volunteers was working like leaven through the entire church, and as he looked from face to face he felt a strange but vivid change of setting, back to the first century when the disciples had all things in common. They were slowly developing the kind of trust in their Lord that the early disciples had as they faced loss and death with courage and even joy. At the close of his message, he asked the church to remember the new life that had begun at Southside Mission.

"We've already lost many of the earlier converts back to the streets," he said. "The pull of drugs and friends has been too much for them to resist. We need to pray that the Holy Spirit will thwart the drug dealers and pimps and gang leaders who deliberately lure people away."

The after-meeting was the largest it had ever been. Jason Clark was one of the few missing, a fact Michael noted without surprise. He and Sharon had spent hours the previous afternoon counseling with Rachel after she had returned, distraught, from breaking off the engagement. Jason had also apparently taken it hard, not even attending the regular church service that morning.

There were many excited questions about the moving of the Spirit at the mission, and several more people offered to help with the ministry. Michael directed them to talk to Jenny Paige, then with a smile asked Roger Paige to stand up.

"Roger was at the mission Friday night, and he asked if he could say something this morning," he explained. "For those of you who don't know him, he's Jenny's son. Roger?"

Roger looked slightly red as he stood up and glanced around at all the expectant, upturned faces.

"This is more embarrassing than I thought it would be," he admitted. The crowd laughed quietly. "I've been going to this church since I was a kid, but it's only been these last few months that I've started really wondering what it was all about. More than anything else, it was because of this pledge thing.

"I'd always thought of God as somehow distant, not connected to real life. But after my mom took the pledge to live her life by asking, 'What would Jesus do?' I started seeing a lot of changes in her. All of a sudden she was doing things I never could've imagined her doing, but she was also happier than she'd ever been before! After awhile it got to me."

He paused to smile ruefully. "I went to the mission the very first night it opened, but I was too proud to go inside. When I went again on Friday, though, I just couldn't help it. There was—there was something—"

His voice faltered, and he hastily blinked back tears. Jenny reached up to take his hand as he went on in a low voice. "There was something there in that room, a kind of love, I guess, that made me feel like a kid. Before I knew it I was at the front bawling like a baby." He took a deep breath. "I guess what I'm trying to say is, thank you. If you people hadn't taken this pledge, I don't think I'd have ever thought twice about how I was living my life."

He started to say something else, then shook his head and sat down. Jenny hugged him as the others clapped and murmured their congratulations.

It was a short meeting, but before the group broke up there were several other confidences. Alex Powell shared that he'd had the joy of leading a co-worker to Christ early that week, and a young newspaper reporter who'd been coming barely a month told how he'd been fired for refusing an assignment that would have required him to spend an evening in a topless bar.

Another young newcomer stood up, trembling, to make a public confession: he had gone that Friday to the owner of the camera shop where he'd worked for more than two years to confess that he'd stolen several valuable cameras in the past, and to arrange to repay the owner for his loss. He'd fully expected to be fired, but to his utter amazement, his boss had kept him on. Even more exciting, though—it had opened the door for him to share *why* he'd confessed his thievery. He and his boss had talked about the Lord for almost two hours.

The First Church group counseled together and prayed for each other, and when they finally went home all of them were filled with the Spirit's power.

Rachel Wingate walked out with Jenny and Roger. Jenny let Roger move a few steps ahead, then put her arm around the younger woman.

"Are you okay?" she asked quietly. "You look a little down today."

"I'm all right. I guess you already know that Jason and I aren't—" She held up her left hand, letting the empty ring finger complete the sentence.

"I heard," Jenny admitted. "Is that why he didn't show up for church today?"

Rachel nodded. "When I left yesterday, he was furious. He accused me of 'betraying his trust' and just about everything else you can think of. Said that if that was the way so-called Christians acted, he wanted no part of it! Can you believe that?"

"I'm afraid I can. I'm actually a little relieved, if you want to know the truth."

"Why?" asked Rachel, a little startled.

"Because I never thought he was right for you. There was always something—I don't know—*false*, about him, like he was playing a part. I was surprised that he took the pledge. I assumed it was probably just for your sake."

Rachel was silent for a moment. "I really thought I loved him," she said painfully. "He was so much fun, and he knew how to make me happy. It was only when I was away from him that I started questioning what we were doing."

Rachel paused, suddenly aware of the amazing changes that had taken place in her thinking. Where would the Lord lead her next?

Even as the Sunday after-meeting was breaking up that day, another meeting in the church was still going strong. It was a small, informal gathering consisting of four deacons, two members of the building committee, the chairman of the foreign missions board, the financial director, and the church treasurer. They had decided to meet in one of the Sunday School rooms where Michael Maxwell wasn't likely to walk in on them.

"I think we're all agreed," Martha Robinson was saying, her pudgy chin quivering with indignation. "Even though this morning's attendance and offering were up compared to the last few weeks, the offering was still down almost 20 percent from what it was seven months ago before Pastor Maxwell started this pledge thing. I think we've been patient enough. If we don't do something now, there might not be a church to worry about in another seven months."

There was a murmur of agreement. "It was Pastor Maxwell himself who said that any church that isn't growing is dying," said Frank Boykin, the financial director. "But when I tried to talk to him about going back to some of our more successful advertising, he just said, 'I've pledged to follow the Lord regardless of the outcome, and I don't believe that's what He would have us do.' He won't listen to reason."

"It's more than that," interrupted John Roberts, one of the deacons. "The biggest thing is, he's concentrating all his time and attention on one small group of people—the ones who've taken his pledge. He's totally ignoring the needs of the rest of the flock."

Martha nodded vigorously. "That's exactly what I thought. Then it's all settled. Frank, are you going to draft the letter to the board?"

"It'll be ready to mail tomorrow. It will probably take them a few weeks to respond, but in the meantime I think we should get the support of a few more of our most prominent families. Maybe we can even start making some quiet inquiries about other pastors that might be interested in taking over."

As they disbanded, the furtive glances and mean-spirited whispers formed a sharp contrast to the spirit of peace that had reigned over the other group just minutes earlier.

It was Thanksgiving weekend, and Rachel Wingate was in Virginia visiting her family. For the first time in almost two months she wouldn't be singing at Southside Mission that Friday night. A choir member from Villa Drive Lutheran Church had volunteered to stand in for her.

There was now a regular contingent of First Church members who faithfully attended the mission each week when Michael preached, including Daniel Marshall, Alex and Cheryl Powell, Connie and 'Menio Garza, Lauren Woods, and, of course, Jenny Paige. Several others, Dr. West among them, came as often as their schedules permitted.

Roger Paige had also faithfully attended since he'd first come forward at the mission. But even though he enjoyed the time of worship and Michael's straightforward messages, he felt increasingly restless. He didn't really fit in with the other First Church members who stayed afterward to pray with and counsel those who had responded to the message.

Even though he was devouring the new "plain English" Bible Pastor Maxwell had presented him the day he was baptized, he didn't yet feel equipped to address the problems many of the southsiders faced. What he really wanted was to find a way to reach other people like himself—the outwardly content men and women who drifted from one club to the next in an endless search for something to fill the emptiness in their lives.

On the way home from the mission that night, he talked to his mother about it.

"It isn't that I don't like the mission," he assured her. "You're doing a great job of reaching people who've slipped through the cracks with traditional churches. But what about people like my friends, Bruce and Dennis, who think church is a joke because of all the hypocrites they read about and see on television? Who's doing something to reach them?"

Jenny looked at her son, a small smile playing at her lips. "It sounds to me like the Holy Spirit might be nudging *you* to do something. Did you have anything specific in mind?"

Roger grinned. "Not really. Right now I'm just complaining! But I know there's got to be a way to get through to them the way you and Rachel got through to me. The problem is, Christians don't usually hang around in nightclubs or bars, so the 'party' crowd rarely sees them. And I don't think many of my friends would even think of coming to church with me. They'd consider it a huge waste of time."

Jenny nodded. "Well, why don't we start praying that the Lord will make it clear to you what you should do? That's the best way I know to come up with some answers."

On that same holiday weekend, several tragedies simultaneously struck the First Church of Ashton.

First, Michael and Sharon Maxwell were awakened early Saturday morning by the insistent ringing of the telephone. Sharon answered it groggily, then, suddenly alert, handed the receiver to Michael. It was Terri Bannister.

She was crying so hard that he could barely make out her words. "Pastor Maxwell, it's Ray," she sobbed. "The kids—we heard a shot in the den and little Bobby ran in to see—Ray's just lying there on the carpet, he's—he's—I don't know what to do! Oh, dear God, I don't know what to do!"

Michael was already out of bed and reaching for his pants. "Terri, I'm on my way. Have you called an ambulance?"

"Jennifer called 9-1-1." She made an obvious effort to control her voice. "Pastor, why—why would he do this? He was going to be baptized tomorrow!"

"I don't know, Terri. Listen, I'll be there in just a minute. Just hang on, okay? Get the kids and go sit in the bedroom until the ambulance arrives."

He wasn't sure if she understood, but when the phone clicked he hung up and turned to Sharon. "I don't know for sure, but it sounds like Ray must've shot himself. Terri and the kids are there alone. Call Jenny and Cheryl and get them to pray, okay? I'll call you as soon as I know what's going on."

At the Bannister's house, Michael walked into a situation out of a nightmare. Paramedics were gathered around Ray's blood-soaked body, carefully lifting him onto a stretcher as two policemen tried to calm a hysterical Terri. One look at Ray's head told Michael that there was no hope for his recovery. The gun he had used was still on the floor.

He had written a short, pathetic note addressed to his wife in his final moments. In barely coherent words, he explained that he'd been involved in an embezzlement scheme at the bank where he worked, and that he'd been alerted by a call early that morning that some of the missing funds had been traced to him. "I've been trying to figure out a way to pay it all back without anyone knowing," he wrote, "but now it's too late. May God forgive me."

Terri clutched the note until a policeman gently took it from her, explaining apologetically that it was evidence. Michael called Sharon, who soon arrived with Cheryl and Jenny. They all stayed with her and the kids until Terri's brother and sister-in-law showed up late that afternoon.

The second near-tragedy occurred that same night, when Martha Robinson's car was violently rear-ended as she sat at a red light. The impact totaled her car and left her with a painful neck injury and two broken toes. Michael received the phone call only moments after he returned from Terri Bannister's house. He went straight to the hospital.

Martha was already recovered enough to be thoroughly enraged at the other driver. "Imagine!" she told Michael, "I was just sitting there minding my own business when this—this *fool* of a woman ran right into me! And she doesn't even have insurance on her car!"

She brusquely waved aside Michael's offers of help. "The doctor says I can go home tonight, as soon as he finishes wrapping my toes. My nephew is coming to pick me up."

"Well, I'm just glad you're okay," Michael said wearily. "Let me know if there's anything we can do for you." He decided not to mention Ray Bannister, although the news would be out soon enough; Martha had a reputation for embellishing stories in the re-telling. Terri would have enough to deal with in the days and weeks to come without any "well-meaning" gossip.

The following morning the *Ashton Herald's* Sunday edition ran a front-page account of Ray Bannister's suicide, mentioning his implication in an embezzlement scheme. Terri didn't come to church. Michael had learned that Ray's funeral date couldn't be set until the investigation and autopsy were complete.

The message he preached that morning was about forgiveness. He chose his text from the Book of Ephesians:

Be kind and compassionate to one another,
forgiving each other, just as in Christ God forgave you.
Ephesians 4:32

"As Christians we tend to talk a lot about forgiveness," he began. "We're very self-righteous about overlooking 'little' sins—'white' lies, angry outbursts, momentary lapses. But the true test is in how we react to the brand new believer who's struggling to overcome a sordid past, or to the older brother or sister in the Lord who stumbles into what we consider *serious* sin—things like adultery, thievery, drunkenness. Do we freely forgive them when they repent, or do we turn our backs on them, leaving them to deal with it alone?

"What would Jesus do?"

He paused, then continued after a moment. "If we're to be imitators of Christ, we need to grasp firmly one central fact: *Forgiving others is a requirement, not an option.* We can't use religious excuses to withhold from others the very forgiveness

God extends toward us. We can't call it 'discernment' when we're passing judgment on people, or cloak damaging slander in the righteous robes of making a 'prayer request.'

"Listen to the instructions Paul gave to the Corinthians about dealing with a brother who had gotten caught up in sin.

> Now instead, you ought to forgive and comfort him,
> so that he will not be overwhelmed by excessive sorrow.
> I urge you, therefore, to reaffirm your love for him."
>
> 2 Corinthians 2:7-8

He rubbed his forehead wearily, then said with obvious difficulty, "We had a new brother who I had planned to baptize today. He came to the Lord with the burden of a past he felt compelled to conceal, apparently hoping to deal with it on his own. When he learned it was going to become a public matter, he didn't have enough confidence in God's—and our—willingness to forgive and stand by him. I pray that we will become the kind of church and the kind of people who are known for our ability to forgive."

After the closing prayer, Michael announced that the regular Sunday after-meeting would be replaced that day by a prayer meeting.

"The Bannister family needs our support, and as some of you know, another of our members, Martha Robinson, was involved in a car wreck late yesterday afternoon. She's not seriously injured, but she's going to have trouble getting around for a while. We need to remember her in prayer as well."

He hesitated, seeming to study their faces. "It's been almost eight months since many of you took the pledge to live one year by asking yourself, 'What would Jesus do?' Looking out over this congregation, I see a number of people whose lives have been radically changed as a result—and their actions, in turn, have affected many others.

"Sometimes when you're following the Lord, you run into some pretty serious opposition. Peter wrote:

Be self-controlled and alert.
Your enemy the devil prowls around like a roaring lion
looking for someone to devour.
1 Peter 5:8

"Now, more than ever, it's time to watch and pray. I hope many of you will stay today."

Most of the people who usually attended the after-meeting remained, joined by a number of others who'd never found time before. The shocking events of the previous day seemed to draw them together, to make them more willing to overlook petty disagreements in an all-consuming desire to seek God's face.

They had hardly begun to pray when the Holy Spirit swept over them, leaving many in tears. Earnest prayers were offered on behalf of Terri Bannister and her children, for Martha Robinson, for Southside Mission, and for the church as a whole. When the final "amen" was spoken, most were astonished to discover that over an hour had passed.

Lauren Woods lingered for a moment after the meeting was dismissed. "Pastor Maxwell," she said, "while we were praying God really laid it on my heart to do something to help Martha. Do you know if she needs help around the house or maybe someone to run errands for her?"

He thought for a moment. "She lives alone, and I think the only relative nearby is a nephew. She'd probably appreciate the offer." He gave her Martha's phone number.

On the way home Michael was unusually quiet. Sharon finally asked him what he was thinking about.

He smiled. "Lauren, actually. Have you noticed the change in her, Sharon? She's not even like the same person anymore. I used to cringe every time she called or walked up to me because she was always so clingy, obviously trying to attract attention to herself. But now it's like she's found her niche. She's turning out to be one of the strongest, most spiritually insightful women in our congregation."

On Wednesday Ray Bannister's body was finally released for burial, and the funeral was held the next day. It seemed to Michael that the entire congregation of First Church turned out for the service, surrounding Terri and her children with a public display of loving support. He could hardly believe it was the same group of people who, just seven months before, had been so scandalized when a feverish young mother had committed the "crime" of disturbing their church service. Now, the disgrace Terri and the kids were having to bear as the result of Ray's actions was being willingly shared by the many, diffusing its devastating effect.

"Did you see what happened there?" Michael later asked Sharon. "The church is finally pulling together, putting aside differences to function as the body of Christ. Did you see John Roberts? He has opposed almost everything I've done for months, but he showed up today and actually asked me if there was anything the family needed." He added thoughtfully, "He stayed for the prayer meeting on Sunday. Maybe that's what finally got through to him."

He was still musing about the changes in the church when the phone rang. It was Dr. Carl Bruce, pastor of the Nazareth Avenue Church in Chicago.

Michael's face lit up when he recognized his long-time friend's deep, slightly raspy voice, but his smile quickly faded when he learned why he was calling.

"Michael," Carl said carefully, "have you had some trouble lately at First Church with the deacons or the financial committee?"

"Nothing outstanding. Just the usual griping I get whenever offerings drop or whenever I've announced that we're changing the way we do things. Why?"

Carl sighed. "I thought it was probably like that. Look, you've got problems—*big* problems—with some of your people. I got a call this morning from a friend on the board; apparently a number of your deacons and some others on the financial committee wrote to them several weeks ago asking for your removal. They accused you of everything but fraud: mismanagement, fanaticism, you name it. My friend on the board who knows we're close asked me to call you and find out what's going on."

The news hit Michael like a physical blow. He sat down slowly, his fingers white as he tightly gripped the phone receiver.

"Michael? Are you there?"

"I'm here. I don't know what to say, Carl. I just came back from preaching the funeral of a new convert who committed suicide last weekend. He left a wife and three children. I was so proud of the church for making such a big effort to turn out to support the family—" His voice trailed off.

Carl waited a moment. "Why don't you just tell me what's been happening at the church the past few months? All the complaints in the letter seem to center on that."

Michael didn't know where to begin. "It all started back in the spring," he said slowly, "when a young woman named Brenda Collier came to our church with her little girl, hoping to find help . . ."

He went on to detail the events that had eventually led to his challenging the congregation to take a year-long pledge to live their lives by asking, "What would Jesus do?" and then told of the many events that had followed, both in his own life and in the lives of other church members.

"I can't tell you what a difference it's made," Michael said, a flicker of his earlier excitement returning to his voice. "It's not only making a difference in our church, but it's spreading out into the community. People who'd never darken the door of a church are being touched because of how His people are acting in business and their family life. One of the most effective preachers in all of Ashton right now is Cliff Bright, who owns Mr. B Food Stores. His commitment to the Lord has cost him a lot, but his life has been a testimony to more people than I can count."

Carl Bruce had listened, fascinated, to the whole story. When Michael finished, the Chicago pastor was openly excited.

"Listen," he said impulsively, "I have an idea. Why don't I drive down to Ashton next weekend and see everything for myself? I can go to Southside Mission with you on Friday night and attend First Church on Sunday. It'll give us a chance to catch up."

"We'll be glad to have you. But while you're here, why don't you plan to preach at the mission Saturday night? The pastor who was scheduled that night called yesterday to say he has to go out of town, so I was looking for a replacement for him."

Dr. Bruce replied quickly, "I'd love to. But I'm not at all sure I'll know how to speak to that kind of audience."

Michael laughed. "It's quite a change from Sunday mornings; I'll tell you that. But it'll be good for you, Carl."

The moment he hung up, Sharon asked anxiously, "What's going on?" From his end of the conversation she'd been able to tell that something serious was happening.

Michael shook his head. "Looks like a lynch mob is forming at church. I've apparently upset some people, and now they've written to the board asking for my removal. A friend of Carl's on the board called and told him about it."

Sharon's lips tightened. "If somebody wants you to leave, why don't they talk to you face to face instead of sneaking around like this behind your back?"

Michael smiled without humor. "It rarely works like that, honey. I've seen it before, even if it's never been directed at me. It starts with a few whispers and complaints and slowly escalates into an ugly feud."

"Just what we need right now," Sharon said glumly. "What are we going to do?"

"I don't know. I think I'd like to talk to Alex and Daniel before I do anything else. The bad thing is, once these things start they almost never resolve peaceably; it only takes a few troublemakers to turn a church upside down. I'd hate to see everything that's been started at First Church destroyed over something like this."

Sharon searched his face. "What if we can't work it out?" she asked, seeing his doubt. "You're not going to let them bully you into resigning, are you?"

Michael sighed. "This is one case where it's hard to know what Jesus would do, isn't it? I just don't know. That's why I want to ask Alex and Daniel, and maybe Cliff Bright, to pray with me. I don't think I can trust my own judgment on something like this."

17

THAT FRIDAY, THE SEASON'S FIRST SNOWSTORM blanketed the city of Ashton. Southside Mission opened its doors four hours early to serve a hot soup lunch to the shivering crowd, many of whom had never been inside. Michael Maxwell and Dr. Carl Bruce carefully made their way downtown at around four o'clock.

Rachel Wingate was already there. Michael introduced her to Dr. Bruce, then asked, "What brings you here so early, Rachel? I didn't expect you until closer to the service time."

"They let us out of class early today because of the storm," she replied. "I knew the mission would be short-handed, so I came straight here. It's a good thing, too; three kitchen workers have already called to say they can't make it." She smiled and held up a wooden spoon. "I'm not much of a cook, but I guess I'm better than nothing. They have me stirring the cheese sauce."

Michael and Carl both laughed. "Michael has been telling me good things about you, Ms. Wingate," said Dr. Bruce.

"He says your singing ministry has touched a lot of people who've become immune to preaching. I'm looking forward to hearing you."

Rachel flushed. "I just hope it goes well. Lots of new people are here tonight because of the storm."

Roger showed up a few minutes later with Jenny. He looked startled to find Rachel in the kitchen.

Feeling his glance, she looked up and smiled. "Well, hello!" she said warmly, brushing a long strand of auburn hair from her face. "What are *you* doing here?"

Roger seemed uncomfortable. "Mom thought they might need an extra hand tonight, so I offered to come in and help." When he hastily retreated from the kitchen, Rachel stared after him with a puzzled expression. What was wrong with *him*?

The service that night was standing room only. Dr. Bruce sat on the front row between Jenny and Roger, listening with interest as his old friend from seminary delivered a down-to-earth sermon that could hardly be called simply a "message"—it was more of a ringing challenge to the wayward to discard their sin-filled lives in exchange for a new life in Christ.

I would never have expected to find Michael Maxwell in a place like this, Dr. Bruce thought. *When I heard him preach two years ago, he'd never have dreamed of using the word 'sin' in a sermon. He was a great speaker, but it never meant much. Now he's different—less eloquent, but also much more powerful.*

At the conclusion of the service, Rachel stood to sing "Amazing Grace." As her sweet voice rang out with the familiar words, she was joined by many in the audience:

Amazing grace! How sweet the sound
that saved a wretch like me,
I once was lost, but now I'm found
'twas blind, but now I see.

Before she reached the second verse, the area around the platform was crowded with weeping men and women. Dr. Bruce quickly joined the other First Church members who moved among the crowd to pray. Within minutes, kneeling with his arm around a black teenager, he found tears streaming down his face as well.

'Twas grace that taught my heart to fear,
and grace my fears relieved!
How precious did that grace appear,
the hour I first believed.

Dr. Carl Bruce preached the next night at the mission. He was amazed to discover that he not only enjoyed it, but that he was effective, as well. He prayed with four people that night.

It was late Sunday night when he finally arrived home in Chicago. Unable to sleep, he sat up in his Nazareth Avenue Church study with pen in hand, searching for the words to effectively describe what he'd experienced that weekend in Ashton. He had returned both thoughtful and agitated.

He decided to write it all down in letter form to his friend on the board, the Reverend Patrick Corridan.

Dear Pat,

It is late Sunday night, but I'm so awake and excited after my weekend visit to Ashton that I feel driven to write to you now, while it's all still fresh in my mind.

As you know, I drove down Friday to spend a few days with Michael Maxwell and to see for myself what effect his actions this past year have had on First Church. Michael and I have been friends since seminary, although our methods have always been rather different. He was always more of a popular "sermonizer," while I tended to be more of a teacher. When he was called to First Church of Ashton within months of graduation, I thought to myself, "They made a good choice. Michael's preaching will fill their pews in record time."

He's now been there almost eleven years, and until about eight months ago he apparently did just that. He took First Church from its small beginnings and aggressively built it into one of the largest and most affluent congregations in the city. The music ministry, which included a full band as well as some very talented vocalists, regularly gave concerts in the community. Michael commanded a rather impressive salary that enabled him and his wife, Sharon, to take exotic vacations every year. It was the kind of position that most pastors—myself included—would consider ideal.

But then, in the spring this year, Michael made a totally uncharacteristic proposition at the end of the service one Sunday morning. He challenged members of the church to volunteer, with him, not to do anything for one year without first asking the question, "What would Jesus do?" As you can imagine, it sent shock waves through that comfortable, well-heeled congregation!

What has happened since then strikes me as so remarkable that I'm not quite sure how to even describe it. Probably the best and easiest way will be for me to tell you about some of the people I met in the church who, along with Michael Maxwell, took what they now refer to as "the pledge."

First of all, Michael tells me he was astonished that several of the most prominent members of the church responded to his rather controversial challenge. One was Ted Newton, the president and general manager of WFBB-TV in Ashton.

Ted has, in less than a year, succeeded in making significant changes in the station's programming to make it a more positive influence in the community. I don't have time to list all the changes, but among other things, he has replaced the most violent and indecent shows with family programming and refused to accept sex-oriented advertising. I understand that Ted is going to be honored in January by a national watchdog group supporting excellence in television.

Another member named Jenny Paige, owner of Paige, Inc., a real-estate development corporation, has devoted a large portion of both her time and money to establish an inner-city church outreach called Southside Mission, which I'll discuss with you sometime soon in more detail.

Cliff Bright, owner of the Mr. B Food Stores chain, has dropped pornographic magazines, tobacco, and hard liquor from all his stores.

Rachel Wingate, the lead female vocalist in the First Church worship team, turned down a lucrative TV movie opportunity several months ago, solely because of her conviction that the part was immoral—not "what Jesus would do."

Although Michael has no idea I know about this, I found out he and Sharon gave up a planned three-week vacation in Italy this year in order to help a family of six they met at the mission. The family had fallen on hard times after the father lost his job, which left them stuck with enormous medical bills for one of their children. The money got them into a clean apartment and bought them a second-hand car so the father could get to and from work. I've never seen a face so transformed with joy as that man's, when he told me what a difference Michael had made in their lives.

The impact of the First Church pledge has also apparently spread beyond their own congregation. At Southside Mission Friday night I met a young man, Keith Walton, who works with Ted Newton at WFBB-TV. His church has become involved with the mission, and he said that his pastor gave essentially the same challenge to their congregation several months ago. He also said he knows of at least two other churches which have done the same thing.

But I'm starting to ramble. What I really want to share with you, Pat, is what I observed as it relates to the accusations you received that Michael Maxwell's "fanatical" actions are causing the church to deteriorate.

In my mind, nothing could be farther from the truth! The fact is, the pledge seems to have resulted in bringing about a new spirit of fellowship in the church that Michael tells me never before existed. He compares it to what the early Christian churches must have experienced, and I can't much argue with him.

There seems to be a genuine sense of caring and interdependency that brings to life the Scripture about the early disciples "having all things in common." It's a refreshing change from the self-centered congregations in so many churches today—including mine!

As for the "deteriorating" condition of First Church, I guess there are several ways of looking at it. From a sheer numbers viewpoint, a case could probably be made that Michael has "scared off" some members. He says they lost about 10 percent of their congregation immediately after he announced the pledge eight months ago, and over the next few months they lost another 5 percent. There is no doubt that this pledge was viewed by many as highly controversial.

Despite the initial loss in numbers, however, the "core" of committed members has remained, and it now appears that the church is once again starting to grow, albeit slowly. At the service this morning, their attendance was the highest it's been since the Sunday when the pledge was first announced.

The main source of discontent seems to rest with a rather small faction in the church who continue to regard those who have taken the pledge as radicals; I suspect it's among those people that you'll find the authors of the letter sent to your board.

Overall, though, their divisive attitude seems to have been held in check by the continued presence of the Holy Spirit in the church, and also by the fact that many of the most prominent members have allied themselves with the pledge movement.

I'm not sure I agree with Michael in everything, but I have to say that what I saw at First Church moves me to strongly re-evaluate my own life and ministry. Although it has been years since I've been moved to tears in church, I found myself weeping both at the Friday night service at the mission and again during the worship service this morning. It wasn't what was said nearly so much as it was that indescribable sense of closeness to my Father. I found myself asking, "How is it that so many of us have let that closeness, that first love, slip away without noticing—without even grieving its passing?"

At any rate, I spent much of my time asking people questions about this "literal imitation of Jesus" the church has embarked upon. Michael tells me that, so far, no one has interpreted the following of Jesus in a way that would compel them to abandon their earthly possessions, give away all their wealth, etc., although several members have, in following their convictions, suffered financial loss. But they're all quick to add that, if anyone were to feel that in his or her particular case Jesus would do that, there could be no compromise. The pledge is to follow Jesus without thought for the results.

I should point out that those who have suffered the loss of either money or job positions have immediately been helped by others in the church. I witnessed part of this myself this morning when I attended the church after-meeting with Michael. A young reporter who'd recently lost his job stood up to share that he had not only been flooded with gifts of money and cards of encouragement over the past few weeks, but that Ted Newton had just found him a job at the TV station!

It was clear, as I looked across the room, that none of those people felt themselves to be alone in their Christian walk. I never dreamed that such close Christian fellowship could still exist today! It left me almost speechless—and, I must admit, more than a little jealous.

Which is why I now come to the real heart of this letter. After we left the church this afternoon, Michael and I talked for several hours about how great an impact this one small group has already had on Ashton and the surrounding communities. And the longer we talked, the more excited we both got.

"What do you think would happen," Michael asked me, "if Christians all across the country made the pledge and lived up to it? What if, in every city and county, just a handful of Christians firmly set their hearts and minds on following Jesus, regardless of consequence? What a revolution it would cause! People would be able to say of us now what they said about the early disciples—that we were 'turning the whole world upside down!'"

From that point on we talked rather wildly, I'm afraid. We imagined encouraging other pastors to form "pledge meetings" like the one at First Church. If their group caused so many changes in just months, how much more could be accomplished with churches all across the country joining the effort, volunteering to simply do as Jesus would?

It would cut the ground out from under those who repeatedly claim that all Christians are hypocrites; instead of having only a few "token Christians" to point to, they'd be exposed to them everywhere—in the workplace, in the schools, in the media, in homes—showing Christ's love by their actions. Can you imagine a more effective message than that?

But this is where I find myself suddenly hesitating. I can't help but ask myself, what would happen if I put this idea to my own congregation at Nazareth Avenue Church? I can think of very few men and women who, to my sure knowledge, would be willing to risk everything they hold dear for such an experiment. Would anyone even respond to the call, "Come and suffer"?

What I saw in Ashton this weekend left me shaken but also deeply hungry for more of the Spirit's power to be manifested at Nazareth Avenue. But I also have to ask, "Am I myself ready to take this pledge?" I dread the question, dread the honest answer. I know that, if I promised to closely follow in His steps, painful changes would be necessary in my life.

At any rate, Pat, I've tried to share my sincere, if somewhat jumbled, thoughts with you about Michael Maxwell and his congregation, and maybe even to leave you with the same dilemma I now face. Should I stand up in front of my people next Sunday and say, "Let's all pledge, from this day forward, not to do anything without first asking, 'What would Jesus do?'" That would undoubtedly startle and upset many people. But why should it?

I'm just not sure I have the courage. Do you?

In Christ's love,

Carl Bruce

18

It was mid-afternoon on Christmas Eve, and Southside Mission was gaily decorated with red and green streamers. In one corner of the dining hall stood a tall, fragrant pine tree, decorated with tinsel and shiny red bulbs.

The smell of turkey and dressing wafted through the rooms, making everyone anxious for the dinner hour to arrive. Outside, the swelling crowd of hungry people overflowed the sidewalks as they jockeyed for position in the food line.

"How does that look?" asked Lauren Woods, centering a pot of poinsettias on the long serving table. Rachel Wingate, holding a silver garland bunched in one hand, stepped back to admire the effect. "Perfect," she replied.

The two young women had been working for several hours to "dress up" the mission for the holiday meal. As they hung decorations and spread paper tablecloths, Lauren had told Rachel for the first time about her idea for a program aimed at helping girls in the south side who'd become mothers at a very young age.

"I'd like to call it 'Parents Too Soon,'" she said. "Some of the girls I've talked to here are only thirteen or fourteen, but they already have one or two babies. They don't have a clue about how to take care of their children; they're only children themselves. I started working with a couple of them—teaching them things like personal hygiene and makeup application—and they just blossomed! So I started thinking; if I could get together with them once a week, teach them some basic 'life skills' like child care and job hunting, and maybe even take them on occasional outings to expose them to a different life, it might break the cycle that keeps them locked into the south side."

Rachel was impressed. "Lauren, that's a wonderful idea! Have you talked to Jenny about it? I'll bet she'd help fund it to start with."

Lauren's face brightened. "Do you really think so? That was my only real concern—I have the time, but I don't have much extra money." She hesitated for a moment before asking, "Would you go with me to talk to her about it? Jenny kind of scares me."

Rachel laughed. "She puts up a tough front, but I don't think I've ever met a softer touch. But I'll still go with you, if that's what you want." She paused to arrange some Christmas napkins in an attractive fan, then asked, "By the way, how's Martha? I heard you'd been lending her a hand ever since her car accident."

This time it was Lauren's turn to laugh. "I don't know whether I've been helping her or driving her crazy, but I've been trying to stop by every other afternoon or so to straighten up her house and make sure she's got plenty of easy-to-cook food in the fridge.

"As far as I can tell, her nephew hasn't done a thing for her, and she's still pretty miserable. She keeps complaining that her neck is getting worse, not better. I don't think she's used to having anyone help her."

"Well, I'm glad you're doing it, anyway. Even if she never thanks you, you're still earning—"

"I know, I know," Lauren interrupted with a smile, "I'm earning 'treasure in heaven.' That's what I keep telling myself. Every time Martha gripes that I don't clean the kitchen the way she does, or that when *she* scrubs the floor it's like a mirror, I'm tempted to walk out and let her try to do it all herself. But—" she shrugged her shoulders, "that's not exactly what Jesus would do, is it?"

Rachel grinned. "No, but it's probably what *I* would do. You must be getting positively *rich* in heaven if you're putting up with that!"

A few minutes later, Jenny and Roger Paige came in. Roger, as usual, disappeared into the other room the instant he saw Rachel. Rachel looked after him with troubled eyes.

Jenny noticed her glance. "Have you and Roger quarreled over something, Rachel?" she asked, puzzled. "I've noticed that he's been rather abrupt with you for weeks now."

"We haven't talked enough to get a chance to fight. The last time I exchanged more than just a couple of words with him was the night he came forward. But then Jason interrupted and dragged me away."

The mention of Jason cast a pall over her lovely face. She had heard several days before that he had accepted a job at a local "men's club"—a high-class topless bar—as a lounge singer. His rejection of God and his faith had been complete.

She took a quick breath and forced herself to smile. "I wouldn't worry about the way Roger's been acting," she added lightly. "It's probably just a leftover from his early childhood. I hear his mother's a real storm-trooper."

Jenny and Lauren both laughed, and the tension in the air disappeared. Soon they were all chatting happily about Lauren's plan for "Parents Too Soon."

But that night, after Jenny got home, she called Roger into her room. Her son plopped down on the small rose-colored love seat in the corner and looked at her inquiringly. She returned his gaze with an equally inquiring look.

"Rachel Wingate," she said carefully, "is an exceptional young lady. I've never met anybody else her age willing to accept responsibility or work as hard for others."

Roger cleared his throat. "Yes, she's a hard worker, all right," he said noncommittally.

Jenny studied him, puzzled. "I don't know many other girls as talented as she is who'd have turned down a movie part because of her convictions, either. Do you?"

"No," Roger answered briefly.

Jenny decided to drop all pretense. "Then why are you being so rude to her?" she cried. "When she walks in a room, you walk out. If she speaks to you, you barely answer. I saw the look in her eyes tonight; you hurt her feelings! Why on earth are you treating her like this?"

Roger jumped to his feet in agitation and began to pace, keeping his back toward his mother. Finally, he whirled to face her. "Don't you know how I *really* feel?" he demanded.

She stared at him, then slowly a look of understanding crept over her face. "You—?"

"I think I fell in love with Rachel that very first night you brought her here," Roger said almost angrily. "I didn't know it at the time, but it was never the same after that. She was different than any girl I'd ever met." His voice suddenly grew soft. "I think what struck me most about her was the—I don't know—the love, I saw in her face. I didn't recognize it then, but it was her love for Jesus."

He paused, then continued after a moment, "If it had been anybody else, any other girl, I would've gone after her, Jason Clark or not. But with her—" His voice trailed off, and he shrugged. "Somehow I just couldn't bring myself to play those kinds of games with her."

"But why haven't you said something since you've come to the Lord? You could at least ask her out instead of treating her like dirt!"

He was already shaking his head. "Don't you understand, Mom? Rachel is—Rachel is *pure*, for lack of a better word. She'd never be interested in someone like me. I mean, I know that in Christ I'm a 'new creature' and all that, but when she looks at me she'll always see a spoiled playboy. She could never take me seriously enough to love me, not in that way."

Jenny didn't say anything. She didn't agree with her son's conclusion, but she knew better than to try to reason with him when he was being hard-headed.

He doesn't realize it yet, she thought, *but he's already being transformed from a moral weakling into a man of strength and courage.* Someday, he might be the very kind of man to whom Rachel would gladly give her heart.

For much of Ashton's young adult crowd, the new year began as many previous years had begun—with drunken partying from club to club. Roger Paige, however, found greeting the new year without his friends at the club a thoroughly disorienting experience. Several people at church had invited him over to play board games or watch videos, but he couldn't work up enthusiasm for the idea. For the hundredth time since his conversion, he found himself thinking, *Aren't Christians allowed to have any fun besides playing Monopoly?*

Sitting up alone late that night, an idea slowly began to form in his mind. After a few minutes, he jumped up and jogged downstairs in search of a notepad and pencil, then fixed himself a sandwich and sat down at the kitchen table.

He thought for a moment, then quickly scrawled:

Celebration Station—A Christian Nightclub
Non-Smoking Soda Bar,
Contemporary Christian Bands, Great Food,
Live Entertainment.

He stared at the words until they became a blur. Was it possible? Could it work?

It was a chilly mid-January morning, Martha Robinson's first Sunday back in church since her accident. She was edging her way down the aisle, trying to keep her still-sore toes from being trampled by other worshippers, when Larry, a suit-clad deacon, approached with a smile.

"Martha!" he said loudly. "Glad to see you back. It's been weeks!"

She gave him a irritable look. "*Six* weeks," she replied with a distinct edge to her voice.

Larry didn't notice. Instead, he pulled her aside. "Listen, have you heard back from the board yet?" he asked, glancing around to make sure no one could overhear. "It seems like they'd have decided *something* by now."

"No, I haven't heard anything," she said uncomfortably. "And really, you know, I've been thinking—" She broke off, obviously reluctant to continue.

"What? What have you been thinking?"

She glanced at him sharply. "Let me ask you this, Larry. During all these weeks I've been out of church, how many times did you visit or even call to see how I was doing?"

"Uh, I—well, Martha," he said uneasily, "you know I work long hours. Besides, wasn't your nephew helping you out?"

"My nephew," she replied coldly, "is useless. In fact, as far as I can tell, most of you who I thought were my friends are useless. The only one in our group who did anything to help me was John. He came over twice and brought groceries."

She adjusted her glasses. "You know who kept showing up all those weeks? Lauren Woods and several others from the pledge group. Pastor Maxwell even found time to come over several times a week. Lauren and the pastor prayed for me each time they were there. I don't know what I would've done without all of them."

Larry looked embarrassed. "I'm sorry, I really am. But that doesn't change the fact that this pledge thing is slowly killing the church. We still need to do something about that."

"Well, I've had plenty of time to think about that. And you know what? I was wrong. The church is growing again—slowly, but it *is* growing. I think we should just let it go."

He stared at her, bewildered, but before he could say anything she quickly added, "I already wrote a letter to the board to tell them how I feel. Now you'll have to excuse me, Larry. The service is about to start."

He watched, open-mouthed, as she slid into a pew next to the Powells. Wait until the others heard about this!

Rachel Wingate was walking into the Ashton Christian Bookstore when a young man burst through the door, almost knocking her down. At her startled shriek, he quickly grasped her elbow to keep her from falling. She looked up to discover that the strong arms supporting her belonged to Roger Paige.

"Rachel!" he said, his clear blue eyes alight. "Are you all right?" But almost instantly that guarded look returned to his face. He reluctantly released his grip on her. "I'm fine," she said. "I was just coming in to buy some sheet music for our concert next month. Where are you going in such a hurry?"

"I have some phone calls to make." He paused, then asked, "Have you talked to my mom lately?"

Rachel shook her head. "We've both been so busy we haven't had much time. Why, what's going on?"

He hesitated again, but the subject seemed safe enough—and he was dying to talk to somebody about it. He decided impulsively to confide in her.

"Well," he said, "a few weeks ago, I got this idea for opening a kind of Christian nightclub, a place where Christians can go on weekends to listen to good music and maybe even bring along some of their unsaved friends."

He held the door open and allowed Rachel to precede him back into the bookstore. As they walked through the aisles together, he excitedly described some of his ideas.

"I found the phone numbers of some local Christian bands that we could book on Friday and Saturday nights," he said, "and I've already talked to a DJ from a Christian radio station who said he'd like to act as emcee. The way I see it, we should have a sandwich menu and soda bar and maybe a bunch of small tables where people could sit around and talk. We could even have a couple of pool tables—but without the haze of cigarette smoke."

His face was transformed by his enthusiasm for the idea. Rachel noticed with approval the new strength and purpose in his manner.

He continued, "If we did it right, I think we could not only reach the 'party' crowd for Christ, but actually make it succeed as a business. Mom and I have been looking at a property in North Ashton that seems just perfect—it already has a small kitchen, hardwood floors for a dance floor, everything. If we can get it for a reasonable price, we're going to buy it."

Rachel exclaimed, "What a great idea, Roger! What made you think of doing something like that?"

He laughed. "Desperation, mostly. It was on New Year's Eve when I was bored stiff. I'm not like a lot of 'regular' Christians, I guess; I just don't fit in with most of the people who teach Sunday School or help out at the mission." He smiled to take the offense from his words. "But the biggest thing is, I keep thinking that nobody is even *trying* to reach the kind of people I used to hang around with! I've been praying about how the Lord could use me to get through to them. I think this might be the answer."

After Rachel paid for her music, she and Roger walked out together. They paused just outside the store, both suddenly stricken with an inexplicable shyness.

"You know," Rachel finally said, "you seem like a totally different person than you were a few months ago. You used to be so smug and cynical, but now you're so much more—I don't know, *real*, I guess, about God and about your life."

He looked embarrassed. "I guess God is working on me little by little, but I still have a lot of catching up to do."

"Maybe not as much as you think. I really respect you for the stand you've taken, Roger, and for your dedication to the Lord."

There was a moment of awkward silence, then he said uncertainly, "Thanks—thanks a lot, Rachel. That means a lot to me." He looked down at her, and their eyes met. In that instant, Rachel read his true feelings for her in his face.

She drove home a few minutes later, aware of a glad, new joy stealing over her. *Roger is everything I kept trying to make myself believe Jason was,* she thought, recalling his animation as he spoke of reaching his old friends for Christ. *I think I might be starting to understand what it means to be loved by a real man.*

And Roger, as he drove home, felt a new surge of hope as he remembered the warm look in Rachel's gray-green eyes.

19

WINTER HAD PASSED AND THE YEAR WAS NEARLY ended—the year Michael Maxwell had set as the time period for the First Church pledge. As the anniversary Sunday approached, several people suggested that it be marked by a special service with a "dinner on the grounds" to follow at a nearby park. Michael agreed that it was a good idea, and preparations were begun.

The past three months had been marked by several notable events, among them Martha Robinson's change of heart toward the whole pledge movement and the budding romance between Rachel Wingate and Roger Paige. On Valentine's Day Sunday, Rachel had come to church with a lovely rose corsage and a radiant smile, holding Roger's arm. Jenny Paige was said to be overjoyed.

The other big news involved the new Christian nightclub Roger Paige had opened in North Ashton. Dubbed "Celebration Station," it had created an instant stir in both the Christian and secular communities.

"This is great!" exclaimed several surprised visitors dragged in by Roger. His friend Dennis even admitted, "I always thought Christian music was old hymns and stuff. But the bands here sound better than the ones at the Mardi Gras!"

Although Zack, the Celebration Station emcee, avoided long "preachy" speeches, he managed to work in quick comments between each song set to point people toward Christ. By the fourth week, the club was regularly packed and starting to show a profit. Several traditional nightclubs, the Mardi Gras included, were even complaining loudly that their business was dropping off. Celebration Station's atmosphere of Christ-like love and joy was proving a formidable rival for the smoke-filled rooms where peace and joy came from a bottle.

Nonetheless, there were still many Christians—Michael Maxwell among them—who found the whole nightclub concept troubling. "Isn't it just 'whitewashing' worldliness to practice it under a Christian heading?" he asked Sharon after attending Celebration Station's grand opening. "It seems a little cheap for Christians to stoop to imitating the world like that—dancing to loud music and drinking 'fake' alcohol."

"I don't think it was exactly worldly, Michael," Sharon protested. "I mean, nobody was talking or dancing in a vulgar way or anything, were they? The song lyrics kind of discouraged that. Were you listening to those girls at the next table? Two of them were telling the other girl about how they'd come to know the Lord since coming to the club. Maybe Roger was right in thinking it would be an effective way to reach the party crowd. You said it yourself when you were talking about preaching at the mission—to reach some people, you have to become enough like them so they can relate.

"Besides," she added mischievously, "if you're going to complain about dancing, you'd better go back and read about King David again!"

"That's not the same thing and you know it," Michael retorted. Her comment made him grin, however, and he finally conceded, "We all agreed not to judge other people's decisions as they tried to follow Jesus as best they knew how. I just hope this doesn't lead any young Christians astray."

With the anniversary Sunday two weeks away, Rachel Wingate came up with an idea.

"I've stayed in touch with the Andersons, little Hallie Collier's grandparents," she told Michael Maxwell. "I was just wondering—do you think we could invite them here for the anniversary service, kind of as a memorial to their daughter?"

Michael nodded thoughtfully. "Good idea. It might be a comfort to them to see what Brenda started here, and what's come of it."

"I'll call them. I just hope they can come; I'd love to see Hallie again. I've talked with her on the phone a few times, and she sounds so cute. She calls me 'Way-tull.' I'll bet she's grown so much in the last year!"

Back at home, Rachel quickly looked up the phone number, and a few minutes later she was talking to Mrs. Anderson.

"Rachel! How are you doing, honey?" Mrs. Anderson was always glad to hear from the young woman.

Rachel explained why she was calling, and after a brief conversation, the Andersons said that they'd love to come to Ashton for the anniversary service. Jenny Paige suggested that the older couple stay with her at the mansion.

Over the next two weeks, the church was filled with a meditative spirit, a sense of quiet reflection about the year now almost gone. Some wondered aloud, "What will happen now that the pledge is ended?" while others looked to the years ahead with renewed excitement. One thing was certain;

none of those who had taken the pledge and kept it faithfully had remained the same.

Michael Maxwell prepared his message for the anniversary Sunday based on the text, "What is it to thee? Follow thou me" (John 21:22, KJV). As he thought back to that day almost a year before when his sermon preparation was interrupted by a stranger at the door, he was struck anew by the changes that had been wrought in his own life. Now, instead of counting on clever phrases or a gripping delivery to bring his messages home, he prayed long and hard for each service to be visited by the divine Presence who could bring life to faltering words, living water to thirsty hearts.

Then, almost before the members of First Church knew it, the anniversary Sunday was upon them. Unlike the morning the year before, it was rainy and overcast; tables for the picnic lunch afterward were hastily moved to an indoor facility. Despite the rain, the sanctuary was filled to capacity. Dr. Carl Bruce had driven down from Chicago at Michael's invitation to attend the service.

As Rachel sang the opening choruses with the worship team, she smiled down happily at Hallie, wedged between her grandparents on the front row with Jenny and Roger Paige. When she finally joined them, she sat next to Roger and held her arms out invitingly to Hallie. The little girl smiled and crawled over Mrs. Anderson to sit on her lap. Roger grinned at her and reached over to tweak one of her small, dark brown braids.

The service that morning was characterized by a spirit of solemn joy that touched—and in some cases puzzled—many first-time visitors. The audience listened attentively as Michael read the story of the rich young ruler, then spoke of "losing your life to find it." He related Christ's call to "come, follow me" to the experiment the church had embarked upon exactly one year before.

"Many of you gathered here today can think back and marvel at the changes that have occurred in your lives and homes as the result of that experiment," he said.

"Many others probably wouldn't even be sitting here today if it hadn't been for someone who demonstrated the love of God toward them."

Epimenio Garza smiled at his wife, then they both glanced over at Cliff Bright. His round face, drawn from the long months of difficulty both at home and at work, brightened momentarily at their grateful nods. On the front row, Roger Paige gently tightened his arm around Rachel's shoulders. Across the church, numerous small smiles and gestures acknowledged lives tightly interwoven by Christ-like love.

"None of us imagined at the time," Michael continued, "all the miracles that would happen, the doors that would be opened, when just a few people started living their lives by one simple rule: asking, 'What would Jesus do?' and then doing it. For many of us, it has been an experience that we are now unwilling to leave behind."

He paused, his eyes resting briefly on Mr. and Mrs. Anderson. "I will always regret that it took a tragedy to wake us up," he said softly. "But now that we're awake, it is my fervent prayer that we'll all continue to live our lives, day by day, week by week, by that same simple rule."

The message was somewhat shorter than usual, but instead of closing with the usual prayer, Michael asked that the congregation spend a few moments in silent reflection, asking the Holy Spirit to move in their own individual lives. In the quiet of that time, a holy reverence settled over the sanctuary; many, sensing the Presence in their midst that went beyond their human understanding, bowed trembling hearts in solemn acknowledgment.

Finally Michael prayed aloud, asking God's continued blessing in their lives as they sought to follow in His steps. Afterward, the audience only slowly stirred, still caught in the glory and wonder of what they'd experienced.

Dr. Bruce lingered behind with Michael long after most of the congregation had left for the picnic area. His face was pale, but determined, as he warmly clasped his friend's hand.

"I made a decision today, Michael," he said without preamble. "I've been wrestling with myself ever since I came here and saw what you and First Church were doing." He paused, shaking his head. "I'm ashamed to say that I've been too cowardly, or maybe too selfish, to take the kind of step you've taken here. I can't imagine my Nazareth Avenue congregation rising to a challenge to make even the simplest sacrifice in their lives, but maybe I'm misjudging them. At any rate, I've decided to go back to Chicago and put it before them."

He met Michael's eyes and found there a strong bond of sympathy. Dr. Bruce smiled grimly before going on, "Now I'd like to ask you a favor. Could I convince you, and maybe some of your people, to come to Chicago and speak to my congregation about what's happened here in Ashton?"

Michael thought about it for a moment, then nodded. "I'll be glad to come, and I can probably get Alex, Cliff, Ted, Jenny, and a few others to come with me. Would three weeks be soon enough?"

"That'll be great. Thanks a lot, Michael, and tell the others thanks, too. I'd like to stay today for the picnic, but I've got to get back to Chicago. Can I call you sometime next week?"

"That's fine. And Carl—," Michael put his hand on the other man's shoulder. "You might be surprised at how your people react. I know *I* was at First Church."

At the picnic that afternoon, Michael was able to talk to everyone but Cliff Bright. Elizabeth didn't care for picnics; at her insistence they'd gone straight home after church. But Jenny, Roger, and Rachel all enthusiastically agreed to go along to Chicago, as did Alex Powell and Ted Newton and their wives. Daniel Marshall and Dr. Patricia West were also interested, but they wouldn't know until closer to that time if they'd be free. They promised to let Michael know.

A few days later, Michael called Cliff Bright at his office. After explaining the purpose of the Chicago trip, he asked the store owner if he could find time to go. Cliff answered quickly that he'd be glad to but added unnecessarily that he doubted Elizabeth would want to come along. The same day Rachel called to let Michael know that the Andersons, at Jenny Paige's urging, had decided to extend their stay in Ashton for the next few weeks, and that she thought they'd like to go with the Chicago group as well.

"The more the merrier," Michael said cheerfully. "I talked to Carl this morning, and now that he's committed himself, he sounds really excited. He's been meeting with a small group of deacons especially to pray for the service, that God will touch people's hearts."

Over the next week, as word spread through First Church about the Chicago church's upcoming "special service," many members made it a point to earnestly pray for the other congregation, and the next Sunday after-meeting at First Church was devoted almost entirely to prayer for a sweeping move of the Holy Spirit at their sister church. As the day grew closer, believers in both Ashton and Chicago prayed as never before, spurred by a deep sense of urgency they only half understood. An unseen cloud of intercession rose to the heavens like sweet incense.

The following Saturday afternoon, Michael and Sharon Maxwell drove to Chicago. Carl Bruce and his wife, Kathy, had invited them to stay overnight so he'd be rested and ready for the service the next morning. Jenny, Roger, and Rachel also drove over that afternoon and checked into a hotel near the church. Most of the others planned to drive up early Sunday morning.

That evening the Maxwells and Bruces enjoyed a quiet dinner, then talked at length about the state of modern Christianity. How had the church in America come to be so far removed from Christ that many lost and dying people could no longer find Him there? How had Christians been lulled into believing that the "way of the cross" could be traded without consequence for lives of greed and self-indulgence?

"Whatever happens in the morning," Carl finally said, "I firmly believe that it's by the Lord's clear leading that I am to challenge this congregation to follow more literally in His steps."

Late that night, long after the others were all asleep, Michael remained wakeful. As he stared up into the darkness, he couldn't stop thinking of all the things he and Carl had talked about. Was it true that the church in America had, for the most part, lost its power to touch and restore the very kind of lost and hurting people which, in the early ages of Christianity, it had reached in the greatest numbers? Was it true that today's Christians would, as a rule, refuse to walk in Jesus' steps if it meant suffering at all for His sake? *Oh, Father!* Michael cried silently into the darkness. *Bring a spiritual awakening to Your people!*

Suddenly, he could no longer stay in bed. He got up and went quietly into Carl's study, where he knelt beside the couch and began to pray. As he continued to intercede for the church, he was filled with an inner agony that left him almost moaning. He had never felt such a deep wrestling in his soul, not even during his strongest experience in Ashton. He prayed, wept, and prayed again, pleading repeatedly for the Spirit to move in the church across the nation.

He spent nearly all that night in prayer, finally rising just before dawn to return to bed for a few hours' sleep.

20

ON SUNDAY MORNING THE LARGE NAZARETH AVENUE Church was crowded to capacity. Michael Maxwell, stepping into the pulpit after his all-night vigil, instantly felt the deep sense of curiosity among the people in the congregation. Most had heard of the Ashton movement, and many of them had come specifically to hear about the First Church pledge and how it had all started. Perhaps a few, at least, had come prepared to mock the whole idea.

But Michael also sensed something deeper, something more serious than mere curiosity, in their faces. He glanced over at Dr. Carl Bruce, sitting on the front row. *There's so much I want to say to these people,* he thought. *Dear Lord, please give me the right words to deliver Your message to them today.*

He started very simply by telling how, just one year before, a stranger had come to his door in Ashton looking for help—only to be turned away. As he painfully related what had later happened to young Brenda Collier, his voice faltered and his hands visibly trembled. Although there was none of the polished eloquence of his former distinctive preaching style, the congregation felt the complete sincerity and humility of a man who has been confronted with a great truth.

"Like many other Christians," he said, "I had allowed myself to become self-satisfied, immune to the hurts and needs of other people around me. I forgot what the Bible has to say about people who practice an empty faith:

"What good is it, my brothers,
if a man claims to have faith but has no deeds?
Can such faith save him?
Suppose a brother or sister is without clothes and daily food.
If one of you says to him,
'Go, I wish you well; keep warm and well fed,'
but does nothing about his physical needs,
what good is it? In the same way, faith by itself,
if it is not accompanied by action, is dead."
James 2:14-17

On the front row, Mr. Anderson reached over to take his wife's hand. They both gazed up steadily at Michael's face.

"I will regret for the rest of my life," he said quietly, "that when Brenda Collier came to my house that day, I wished her well and sent her away empty-handed. But I can truly say today that, because of her tragedy, Ashton has seen a spiritual reawakening which has already changed the lives of countless people."

He went on to tell how he had come to challenge his own church to join him in pledging for one year to do as Jesus would do, then shared some of the results at First Church.

"I'm sure many of you here in Chicago are already aware of the dramatic programming changes made this last year at WFBB-TV," he said, "but you might not be aware that those changes came about solely because of the station manager's pledge to live his life by asking, 'What would Jesus do?' and then doing it." He nodded slightly at Ted Newton in the audience. "That decision has already provided a living testimony of God's love to countless other people, including eighteen children who've found permanent adoptive homes through Channel 5's new 'Wednesday's Child' program.

"Another result many of you will probably recognize is the removal of all pornographic magazines, tobacco products, and hard liquor from the Mr. B Food Stores chain. Those changes have cost the owner a great deal of money, and recently the loss of two entire stores, but it has also provided a testimony in the community that has already resulted in lives being transformed." In the audience, Cliff Bright looked down self-consciously.

"I could give example after example. Southside Mission that has, in barely eight months, seen more than seventy-six men and women make decisions for Christ, was started by two women who believed Jesus would use their money and talents to shine a light in the darkness of downtown Ashton. The weekly prayer group at Vickers Regional Airport that now numbers more than one hundred was started by a manager who believed Christ would treat His employees with both fairness and love.

"But for every one of these 'big' success stories, there are many, many more 'small' stories, where just one person, by simply acting as Jesus would in an everyday situation, has touched someone else's life in a significant way."

He paused to look down at little Hallie, who was bouncing happily on Roger's leg. As he lifted his eyes to briefly gaze across the audience, there was an almost studied stillness in their faces.

"Several weeks ago, I baptized a young man who had a strange story to tell about how he came to know the Lord. It seems that he was driving his rather beat-up car one day not long ago when he ran out of gas and had to pull off the road. Since he didn't have a gas can, he got out and started pushing the car along toward the nearest gas station, which was almost a mile away.

"But he'd gone only a short distance when another car carrying a well-dressed young couple pulled up beside him. To his astonishment, the other man immediately called out, 'Here, let me help you!' and jumped out to push from behind. Together, they pushed the car all the way to the gas station, the young woman driving along behind them with her hazard lights flashing.

"But that wasn't all. When they finally got the car up to the gas pump, the well-dressed young man, whose clothes by now were sweaty and dirty, asked the other man, 'Can I fill it up for you?' apparently concerned that he might not have any money with him.

"The first young man was so bewildered by all that had happened that he blurted out, 'Why are you doing all this for me?'"

Michael smiled, not seeming to notice a flushed young couple—Roger and Rachel—sitting on the front row. "You can guess at the reply. The young couple who had stopped to help the stranger had both taken the pledge to live every day by asking themselves, 'What would Jesus do?' and then doing it."

He fell silent for a moment, sensing the Spirit's presence in the quiet sanctuary. When he continued, it was in a thoughtful voice.

"The point is, it's rarely the great sermons or extravagant programs that reach people for Christ. More often than not, it's the Christian homemaker who takes a meal to a neighbor who's ill; the Christian teenager who mows an elderly widow's yard; the Christian father who makes time to spend with the child of an overworked single mother. It's those individual acts of sacrificial love that not only change other people's lives but also bring great joy to the giver.

"In Matthew, Jesus used two parables to illustrate the Christian lifestyle:

"'The kingdom of heaven is like treasure hidden in a field. When a man found it, he hid it again, and then in his joy went and sold all he had and bought that field.
Again, the kingdom of heaven
is like a merchant looking for fine
pearls. When he found one of great
value, he went away and sold everything
he had and bought it.'
Matthew 13:44-45

"Jesus never preached that following Him would result in a carefree, comfortable existence; to the contrary, He talked about people who willingly gave up *everything they had* for His sake! But the point is, the sacrifices were all for a purpose, not just for the sake of suffering—and the end result was always great joy."

He carefully closed his Bible. "Over this last year, many of us in Ashton who took the pledge to live our lives by asking, 'What would Jesus do?' have been accused of being radicals and religious fanatics, of having gone too far in our attempts to literally follow in Jesus' steps. It appears that today's church, the church that is called after Christ's own name, can come up with a million excuses for not following Him if it might mean inconvenience or personal suffering. We think we're somehow entitled to our ease and comfort, that we're doing something special if we donate to a worthy cause or sit on a committee. But I think one of our First Church members put it very clearly," his eyes went briefly to Jenny Paige, "when she posed the question: 'Is it really following Jesus to give away something you'll never miss?' We forget that the only sacrifice God finds pleasing, the only sacrifice that touches people around us, is when we give *ourselves.*"

Michael took a deep breath and looked out at the audience. "I want you to think with me for a moment," he said, "about what would happen if today, in this very church, Jesus were to stand here and call some members to do just what He asked of the rich young ruler—to give up their wealth and literally follow Him? Could they do it? What would happen if he called others to run their businesses in ways that, while less profitable, would bring Him more glory? Would they be willing? *What, today, is the test of Christian commitment?* Isn't it exactly the same as in Christ's own lifetime, when He said, 'Any of you who does not give up everything he has cannot be My disciple'?"

The congregation sat motionless, their eyes riveted on Michael's strong, passionate face.

When he continued, it was in a low voice, almost a whisper.

"Can you even imagine," he said, "what would happen if every Christian here in Chicago woke up tomorrow morning and suddenly began to do as Jesus would do? It staggers the mind! What would Jesus do about the many homeless families, mothers abandoned with small children, who live miserably in group shelters downtown? Would He turn His back on them? Claim it was none of His business?

"What about the low-income housing projects, where men and women live in desperate hopelessness, believing drugs and alcohol are their only respite? Would Jesus stand idly by, allowing a tidal wave of evil to sweep them away?

"What would Jesus do in the middle of a society that races so hard after money that they don't have time or energy left for their spouses and children? What would He say about the soft, selfish lives many of His people lead while turning a deaf ear to the cries of penniless missionaries? Would He do nothing, say nothing, feel nothing?

"I believe that it's time for a new commitment to Christian discipleship, following Jesus like the early church did without regard for cost or sacrifice. If our definition of being a Christian is simply to enjoy a good, comfortable life surrounded by friends and luxuries while steadfastly avoiding the pain and trouble of the world around us—if that's our definition of Christianity—then I'm afraid we're a long way from following in the steps of the One who was called a 'Man of sorrow'; who sweat, as it were, great drops of blood; who cried out as He hung in anguish upon a rough cross, 'My God! My God! Why hast thou forsaken me'!"

When Michael Maxwell finished his sermon and bowed his head, a great silence fell over the congregation. Into the silence, there slowly came the sound of muffled sobs—and a consciousness of the divine Presence that left the people trembling. Although many had expected Michael to ask for volunteers to pledge to do as Jesus would do, he didn't utter a word. He just remained standing at the pulpit, eyes closed, head bowed in silent prayer.

Then, unbelievably, there followed a scene that neither Michael Maxwell nor Dr. Carl Bruce would ever have imagined occurring at the fashionable Nazareth Avenue Church. One by one, men and women quietly rose and slipped out into the aisle to make their way to the front. When Michael finally looked up, he was surrounded by a crowd of people offering their earnest promises to do as Jesus would do. It was a spontaneous movement prompted by the Holy Spirit, not by a clever or persuasive sermon. Michael saw, in that joyous moment, all his prayers of the night before being answered far beyond his wildest hopes.

Then he noticed Mr. and Mrs. Anderson frantically beckoning to him. They were standing at the front, their arms around a sobbing, painfully thin, young black man. Michael made his way over to them.

"Pastor Maxwell," Mrs. Anderson said tearfully. "Do you know who this is? It's Jim, Hallie's father."

Michael stared incredulously, taking in the young man's gaunt, stricken face. *How—?*

With obvious difficulty, Jim Collier turned to face Michael. "I think I talked with you on the phone once a long time ago," he said in a low voice, "but I was so high I don't remember much about it. There were whole weeks back then that went by in a fog." He drew a ragged breath. "Then yesterday I ran into Tim Mott, a guy I used to buy dope from down in Ashton. He started telling me about how he's into this Jesus thing now, working as a counselor at Southside Mission. He bought me lunch."

He looked down, embarrassed. "I hadn't eaten in a long time; I got caught with some pills last month and lost my job. Anyway, Tim told me my—the Andersons would be here today with Hallie. I just thought—I don't know. It had been a long time, and I just decided—" He stopped, unsure of what to say.

Mr. Anderson said quietly, "He came to see Hallie, Pastor Maxwell, but the Lord touched him during the service. He says he wants to turn his life over to Christ."

Michael searched the older man's face, seeing the deep pain reflected in his dark brown eyes. This was the young man who had callously abandoned their beloved daughter, ignoring all his responsibilities in his lust for drugs. Only the power of the

Holy Spirit could put it in their hearts to tolerate, much less forgive, such a man.

Just then, Jenny Paige quietly joined them. "Pastor Maxwell, Dr. Bruce asked us to stay after the service to help counsel with the people who came forward today. He's moving everybody into the church conference room." She gave the Andersons a reassuring smile; over the two weeks that they'd been her guests at the mansion, they had spent many hours talking about the Lord. Now, they walked as a group to the conference room, where more than seventy people were already waiting.

That was a remarkable day in the history of the Nazareth Avenue Church. Michael Maxwell and his small band from First Church stayed long into the afternoon, talking and praying with those who'd come forward. In many ways, the after-meeting that day resembled many of those they'd experienced in Ashton. Many church members solemnly took the pledge to do as Jesus would do, and toward the close of the meeting the Holy Spirit moved upon those gathered there, leaving them filled with almost indescribable joy.

Afterward, the First Church group ate lunch with Dr. Bruce and his wife. Cliff Bright, Ted and Kim Newton, Roger and Jenny Paige, Rachel Wingate, and Alex and Cheryl Powell were all there along with Michael and Sharon Maxwell. They spent the meal in a joyous recollection of the morning's events. Jenny shared that the Andersons had decided to stay overnight in Chicago while they talked further with their former son-in-law. Jim Collier had prayed that day to accept Christ as his Lord and Savior; rising from prayer, his tear-stained face had been literally transformed with joy. He was anxious to learn more about his new Lord, and had asked Dr. Bruce to baptize him that very night.

It was late that evening when Michael and Sharon finally arrived back home in Ashton. Long after Sharon went to bed, however, Michael sat up in his study, thinking over, once again, all the experiences of the last year. As he reflected on all the changes that had come to his life as he had tried to follow Jesus more literally, he was conscious of a deep stirring in his spirit, a call to prayer. He finally slipped out of his chair and knelt beside it, resting his head wearily on his hands.

Almost immediately, he experienced a vivid waking dream in which he saw distinctly a series of future events—a vision planted in his heart and mind and soul by his Creator.

He saw himself going on to live his daily life in a simpler, more unselfish fashion, increasingly willing to reach out to those around him in need. He also saw, more dimly, that the day would come when the divisive element in his church would grow stronger, causing him to suffer more as he increasingly sought to imitate Jesus and His conduct.

My grace is sufficient for thee, he heard through it all.

He saw Rachel Wingate and Roger Paige married, melding their lives and youthful talents in joyful service to their Lord. Roger he saw continuing to minister to the affluent "party" crowd, while Rachel's pure voice sang on into the darkness of sin and despair at Southside Mission, eventually, he saw dimly, to reach far beyond Ashton to draw lost souls all across the nation to Christ.

He saw Alex Powell continuing to work faithfully in a job not to his liking, but shining ever brighter as a witness for Christ because of his attitude of genuine humility and loving concern for all those around him.

He saw Cliff Bright suffering even more harshly in his marriage and meeting with additional business reversals, but growing through his suffering into a deeper knowledge of his Master and emerging from his reverses with Christian honor and integrity that would become an example in the community.

He saw Ted Newton defining a new, more responsible approach to television programming that would, in time, come to be recognized as a leading force in the nation, eventually spawning similar programming changes in television stations across the country.

He saw Ashton Christian College president Daniel Marshall becoming embroiled in national controversy because of his outspoken conviction that Christian students should minister to the world physically as well as spiritually, considering a Christian influence in such "secular" fields as the arts, journalism, literature, and film and television to be as important for the kingdom of God as pastoral ministry or foreign missions.

He saw Jason Clark, who had coldly turned his back on his faith, rising to national fame as a composer, writing cynical songs that, while popular, dripped with scorn for everything he'd once claimed to hold sacred.

He saw Lauren Woods continuing to work with young unmarried girls in Ashton's south side, growing in both wisdom and grace as she found, in following Christ, the fulfillment she had once believed could only be found in a man.

He saw Dr. Bruce ministering to his Nazareth Avenue congregation for a time, then resigning to begin a new ministry among Chicago's roughest housing projects, where he would fearlessly venture into the dull, dark, terrible places with the good news of Christ's redemption.

He saw Jim Collier and Tim Mott and a great crowd like them redeemed and giving in turn to others, living testimonies to the reality of the new life Christ offers, even to the most hopeless and ruined of people.

And then he saw a familiar figure, One whose face shone ighter than the sun as He beckoned with nail-scarred hands.

Somewhere an angel choir was singing, and there were many voices and triumphant shouts of joy. The figure of Jesus grew more and more splendid, until Michael felt he had to avert his eyes.

"Lord Jesus!" he cried, still not sure if he was speaking aloud or in a dream, "open our eyes to the needs of the world around us! Let Your church begin to follow You more faithfully! Refocus our lives so Your Spirit can do His work in the world through us."

When he rose at last, weary but joyful, Michael felt, as never before, the weight of human sin and misery in the world, and the great responsibility of the church to penetrate the darkness by allowing God's love to shine through His people's lives.

And with a deep sense of both awe and gratitude, Michael Maxwell went to bed to dream of a church renewed, a church "without spot or wrinkle," obeying Jesus joyfully, following closely in His steps.